REVOLT ON THE CLYDE

REVOLT ON THE CLYDE

CLYDE

An Autobiography

William Gallacher, M.P.

Introduction by Michael McGahey

LAWRENCE & WISHART
LONDON

First published Spring 1936
Second Edition November 1936
First Published in the Workers' Library July 1940
Reprinted July 1941
Reprinted September 1942
Third Edition 1949
Fourth Edition 1978, with Introduction by Michael McGahey

© Lawrence & Wishart Ltd

Printed and bound in Great Britain at
The Camelot Press Ltd, Southampton

CONTENTS

v

INTRODUCTION

The name of Willie Gallacher is still spoken by many miners with pride in the knowledge of having known him, having heard about him, or having had the opportunity of reading his works.

Willie Gallacher was a foundation member of the Communist Party, and before the formation of the Party in 1920 he had already spent a lifetime of service in the Labour and Trade Union Movement.

No one can speak of the Red Clydeside, the militant Shop Steward Movements, the establishment of the Rent Restriction Acts, or the great anti-War Campaigns of 1914/1918 without Gallacher emerging as a powerful and leading figure. His name is closely linked and allied to great figures of the Scottish and British Labour Movement, such as John McLean with whom Gallacher stood shoulder to shoulder in the fight against the imperialist war of 1914/1918.

It was Gallacher who more than any other recognised the power of the Shop Stewards' Movement and how it was able to mobilise the workers on the Clyde, bringing to bear great pressure, not only on the official right-wing leadership of the Trade Union Movement at that time, but also on Governments, defending the interests of the workers and repulsing the attacks of the employers who were utilising wartime opportunities to attack the living standards of Trade Unionists.

Gallacher was a powerful propagandist, an agitator who had perfected the skill of platform oratory.

Those of us who had the privilege of knowing him will always remember his ability to simplify the most complex situation, explaining things in terms that were easily understood by ordinary workers.

Following the foundation of the Communist Party in 1920, Gallacher saw the need to use Parliament as a tribune on behalf of the people, never forgetting to draw attention to the importance of extra-parliamentary activity. His experience as chairman of the Clyde Workers' Committee, which became a model for militant shop stewards, many of whom fanned out into different sections of the Labour Movement, enabled him, when campaigning to become Communist Member of Parliament for West Fife in 1935, to appeal to the Movement, not only to win more Communists in Parliament, but to maintain mass pressure on the parliamentarians.

Gallacher's name is indelibly linked with the miners of Fife, and today one can travel through the Scottish coalfield and few, if any, are the villages where his name is unknown. Older miners speak with pride of how Willie spoke in this welfare centre or that hall, and how he inspired them in the days of grave difficulties when the miners were isolated and facing the rapacious attacks of the coalowners. Gallacher, with his close mate, Abe Moffat, who became President of the Scottish Miners, was always there defending and advancing the interests of the miners.

Gallacher was an example of a deeply-read, cultured working-class leader and this book, which was a must for people of my generation, I hope will be widely taken up in the Movement. In it we have the story of a powerful leader against the background of the great events that led up to and followed the First World War, events that need to be continuously analysed as they hold so many lessons for those of us active today in the Labour and Trade Union Movement.

MICHAEL McGAHEY
President of the National Union of Mineworkers (Scottish Area)
May 1978

CHAPTER I

MY object in writing this book is to tell of my experiences in the working-class struggle. I do not intend to go into intimate details about my family and my childhood. Insofar as I touch upon these things at all it will be only to mention one or two incidents in my early life that had a definite bearing upon my becoming a working-class agitator.

I was born—the fourth of seven children—in the famous thread town of Paisley, on Christmas Day, 1881. My father was Irish, my mother a Highlander. The former died when I was seven years old.

My mother, who had to work hard while my father was alive, had to work still harder after his death. She went out washing and had to slave for every penny she got. Often, on my way back from school, I would go and meet her coming from her work and accompany her home. I used to feel it a terrible thing that my mother should have to toil so endlessly. I made up my mind that as soon as I could work for her she should go out washing no more.

I got my first job when I was ten years old—carrying milk-cans every morning from six till about half-past eight. For this I was paid a shilling and a few coppers every week. What joy it was when first I could give my mother something towards my keep.

When I reached the age of twelve I left the school for ever and got my first full-time job, as a grocer's boy. I was a willing worker, a fact of which my new boss took full advantage. I spent my days carrying heavy loads, but I enjoyed it. It was only my capacity for hard work that saved me from early dismissal, for I could never stomach speaking to my " betters " with the deference my employer thought I should assume.

But the limit was reached one Tuesday—my half holiday. On my way home on that day I was used to carry a large basket of provisions to the home of my employer's sister-in-law. As her house was on my way home I never objected to this. Her son, my employer's nephew, was himself an assistant in the shop.

On this particular Tuesday however, just as we were putting the shutters up, a load of smoked hams was delivered at the shop. " Wait a minute," said the boss, and he opened the load and took out a ham, which he started to bone and string up.

I waited in growing impatience to get on my way, not for one minute but for quite a considerable time. It was nearly half-past two when the boss finished. He then came to me with the ham, put it in the basket beside me, and instructed me to deliver it to a customer who had it on order.

This meant going a long way out of my road

home, so I looked up and said to the boss: " Do you know I finish at two on Tuesdays?" I have never seen a man look more astonished than he did then. " What do you mean?" he gasped. I told him I meant that I would deliver the groceries as usual, but not the ham.

He looked at me as if I were some unusual kind of insect and burst into a storm of abuse. But I stood firm. He gave me up as hopeless and tried new tactics. " Go out and get another boy," he yelled at his nephew.

I was very young, but not too young to see through bluff of this sort. You can't find boys who will " deliver the goods " hanging about on street corners. But the nephew went dutifully out.

" Are you going to deliver them or not?" the boss asked in a threatening tone. I repeated what I had said before. " Then, out of here," he shouted. So I got out.

The nephew was waiting outside for me. He pleaded with me to go back and take the load. " If you don't," he groaned, " I'll have to." This did not worry me greatly. " I'll take the usual lot," I said once again, " but nothing else." I then went home.

When I told my mother what had happened she just shook her head. She couldn't understand very clearly what it was all about, but she always had a belief that " oor Wullie'll no' go far wrong." This was the first time I had serious trouble with an employer.

I went back to the shop next morning. " What do you want? " shouted the boss. " I want my money," I replied, " at the same time I'll carry on if you like till you get another boy." Believe it or not, I held that job down for months after, just as if nothing had happened. But I was never asked again to stop after recognized closing hours.

As soon as I was fourteen I left the grocer and got a job in a sanitary engineering shop. Soon after this I took up with the Temperance movement, having an awful, deep-seated hatred of the booze. This arose from my family, especially my mother, having suffered horribly from my father's over-addiction to alcohol. He was a good husband and an exceptionally affectionate father, and in the later years of his life mastered the booze craving completely.

I might mention here that my father was one of the last men to be branded on the back for desertion from the Army. He deserted to be near my mother when she was very ill. For that the branding-iron was used on him, and he carried a burned-in D between his shoulders for the rest of his days.

When anyone saw it and asked what this " D " denoted, my father would shrug his shoulders and reply, " For dacency." I was still very young when my father died, but my eldest brother was already a young man. He was my mother's favourite child. She was fond of all of us, but how she adored the oldest boy! When he developed a weakness for alcohol it almost drove her crazy. Her suffering was so acute that I used to clench my boyish fists in rage every time I passed by a pub.

In my new job I had a desperate desire to make good and get my mother away from the washtub as soon as possible. I was nineteen before this was possible, but by then the joint earnings of my sisters and myself enabled my mother to give up her back-breaking toil. But the long years of arduous labour had been too much for her. A few short months later, at the early age of fifty-four, she collapsed and, after a few weeks' illness, died.

Just a typical tragedy of working-class life. A tragedy I have seen repeated many times in workers' homes. Nevertheless, a tragedy I shall never forget. To the last my mother adored her eldest son; to the last she maintained—even though in her latter days I was reading " strange " (Socialist) books—" Oor Wullie'll no' go far wrong."

But although a keen student of Socialism, always arguing in whatever factory I was working, as late as 1906 when I was twenty-four years of age, I refused to support Bob Smillie's parliamentary candidature in Paisley, because he was a director of a Public House Trust. The young woman who was later to become my wife was an ardent supporter of Smillie and nearly broke her heart at his defeat. If she could have got at me then she would have broken my head.

The election over, I learned to my disgust that those self-same colleagues of the Temperance movement who had weaned me from Smillie by talk of

his association with the Trust, had been busily at
work during the election supporting the candidature
of Sir Thomas Glen Coats in Renfrewshire, in the
full knowledge that he was associated with a similar
Trust. That finished me with the organized Temperance movement. I severed my connection with
it and looked around for new associates.

I joined the Paisley branch of the Independent
Labour Party, which made another new member on
the same night. His name was Pat Machray. We
became the closest of friends and quickly found ourselves reacting similarly to our new surroundings.
They smacked too much of the Sunday School.
They were too much like what we were both trying
to get away from.

We searched around for something more suited
to our temperaments, and discovered a small group
of Marxists who met in a cobbler's shop. We joined
up with them and soon a branch of the Social Democratic Federation was in full swing. Machray and I
were on the platform every Sunday night. I was
a heavy, slogging sort of speaker, putting all I had
into the propaganda of socialism. But Machray
had a touch of genius. His speeches, even in those
early days, were a compound of wit and brilliance.

He kept up a constant string of controversies in
the local paper—the Paisley *Daily Express*—and his
letters were of a character that a mere mention on
the poster of a " Letter from P.M." was sufficient
to guarantee the edition selling out. Added to these
gifts, he had great skill with a pencil and given the

opportunity might well have become an outstanding cartoonist.

Alas, driven by necessity, Pat took a job on the Gold Coast. Ten months later he returned to Scotland broken in health. Two months after his return he died. I sat all night with him as he gasped out his life. We had been very close and dear comrades and it was agony to watch him passing. So bright he had been, so rich in ideas, so capable of doing great things for the cause to which he was devoted; yet he was crushed out of existence in the very struggle to maintain it.

Through the Social Democratic Federation I came into contact with John McLean, whose fine revolutionary fervour made a great and lasting appeal to me, and played a great part in determining the course of my life.

1909 was a year of great unemployment in Scotland. I had trouble with the foreman on the job, trouble which ended with my getting the sack. I started hunting for another job, but none could I find. The country was going through an unemployment crisis which resulted in the introduction of the Insurance Acts a year or so later.

Just as I was getting desperate I ran across an old pal who was a steward on a transatlantic liner. After a talk with him I went to the docks and tried to get a ship. When a ship docked the stewards " worked by," loading up provisions, bedding and other things associated with their department. Often extra hands were taken on for this work. I got an occasional job of this kind before succeeding in getting signed on as a steward with the Allan liner, *Laurentian*.

The job was awful—cleaning, scrubbing and serving food. I was soon in trouble with my colleagues because I had refused a tip. They had to rely on tips to make up their wages, and they were naturally always on the look out for them. But I could never accustom myself to accepting them. The very idea of holding out my hand was repugnant and, in addition, most of the passengers I came in contact with were very poor and obviously needed every penny they had to make a start in their new life. However, that is by the way.

Boston was reached. Passengers and cargo were unloaded and we got ready for the return trip. We left Boston on a Friday. On Sunday afternoon we ran into a thick fog. All night we went steaming through it with but the vaguest notion where we were. At 5.30 on the Monday morning the ship came to an abrupt stop. We had crashed into a reef off the Newfoundland coast. We hadn't many passengers aboard, fortunately, so with some difficulty we got them into the boats; with still greater difficulty we found a place where we could land.

The cove where we landed was used as a fishing station in the summer and there was a group of huts there which provided us with shelter till we were picked up by a Newfoundland boat on the Tuesday afternoon, and taken to St. Johns. While waiting to be picked up I learned that, according to the

Regulations, the company could stop our pay from the t:me the ship struck, no matter when we got back. But, everyone was confident the Allan Line would pay up for the whole duration of the voyage.

On Tuesday afternoon when the *Prospero* lay off the cove to pick us up, we loaded the passengers and their baggage in the boats and rowed them out. As soon as we got aboard we got tea, bread and margarine and bully beef. We cleared the tables in record time. We had to remain at St. Johns a week before we were picked up by the Allan liner *Mongolian*, which took us back to Glasgow.

Arrived at Glasgow we were handed our pay sheets just before leaving the ship. What a shock! Eighteen days' pay! Our pay stopped from the moment the ship had struck the reef! I, for one, could scarcely believe my eyes. Eighteen days at 2s. a day. Thirty-six bob, from which I had to pay 17s. 11d. for the clothes received before leaving, clothes that were necessary for the job.

I got a number of the boys together and proposed that we make a fight of it. I pointed out that we had been under orders, and had carried out orders on the Tuesday, when we carried the passengers and their baggage to the *Prospero*. But the boys wouldn't face up to it.

The next day we had to return to the *Mongolian* to sign off. We formed up in a queue and proceeded through the saloon where the chief purser and several other officers were seated with the representative of the Board of Trade. One by one we were paid what money was coming to us and were duly signed off.

When it came to my turn I put down my wages sheet, and pointing to the deductions, asked, " What do you mean by this? " They all stared at me, then the purser barked, " What do you mean? " " I mean," I replied, " that thirty-six bob is due to me from the company, and thirty-six bob is what I want."

The purser tried a tone of sweet reasonableness. " But," he said, " you've got to pay for the goods you've had."

" All right," said I, " but that's my business and you can leave it to me. In the meantime the Company owes me thirty-six shillings and I don't sign off till I've got the thirty-six shillings."

That seemed to stump him. The purser looked to the Board of Trade man for assistance in his plight but received none. As the latter sat silent I thought I had better give him a jog. " You're here," I said, " to see that we get proper treatment, so please get me thirty-six shillings."

By this time the purser had somewhat recovered his composure and said: " Well, we can't do anything here about it. You'd better come to the office on Monday." I passed through the saloon without signing off. On the deck the boys gathered round me. " You won't get anything by this," was the general tenor of their remarks. " Well, I won't sign off until I do," I replied.

On Monday I went to the office in Bothwell

Street good and early. I sent my name in and the manager came out. In full view and hearing of the clerks he started to tell me what he thought of me—and it wasn't much. I retorted in kind, so he sent for the police to have me removed. Two policemen came and persuaded me to leave. I made my way down to the docks and had to stand a lot of chaff from the boys who were hanging around for another ship. But at two o'clock a clerk came down from the office looking for Gallacher. The Shore Superintendent wanted to see me, I was told.

So to see the Shore Superintendent I went. " I hear you made an awful scene up at Bothwell Street," he said. I told him I had only handed back what I was getting. " But," he said, " it was a mistake to lose your temper. Now if you were to go up again I'm sure it would be all right."

I understood what that meant, so to Bothwell Street I went once more. As soon as they saw me the clerks started whispering, obviously hoping I had come to bring a little more excitement into their dull lives. But they were doomed to disappointment. Instead of the Manager out came the purser, who asked me to go to the Board of Trade with him, assuring me that everything was now settled.

At the Board's office I was given the thirty-six shillings, the deductions were struck off my wages sheet and I signed, signing at the same time my finish with the Allan Line.

When I showed the boys on the dock-side my thirty-six bob and my wages sheet, they nearly went cock-eyed. Their only consolation was the belief that I would never get another job out of the Port of Glasgow.

But the next day I was down on the docks good and early, having heard that the *California*, an Anchor Line boat, was in from New York. An enormous crowd of unemployed seamen had also arrived with the hope of getting signed on. Included among them were most of the stewards who had been with me on the *Laurentian*. I found out the name of the Chief Steward—a Mr. Wheat—and made as if to walk off the dock. A few minutes later I came back running as fast as I could to the *California*. I went up the gangway at a fine pelt. To the seaman on watch at the top of the gangway I said breathlessly: " I've a most important message for Mr. Wheat, where can I find him ? " He directed me and I knocked at the door of the Chief Steward's room.

On entering I found a pleasant-looking man sitting in a very comfortable cabin. He got up as I entered and offered me a seat. I opened with : " Have you heard, Mr. Wheat, that the *Laurentian* was sunk a couple of weeks ago ? " This was news to him and he was immediately interested. I told him about the wreck and expressed the hope that he would forgive me for breaking in on him. I went on to explain the difficulty I had had in getting signed on in the first instance, and how, after my

first trip, I was on the stones once more. He asked
me a few friendly questions, then told me to come
up the following day and "work by," promising
that he would see that I was signed on with the old
hands on Thursday.

So, on the Saturday, much to the disgust of my
Laurentian colleagues, I went sailing off once more.
But I never took to the sea and after several winter
voyages in the wildest weather I packed it up and
once more started the hunt round the Glasgow
workshops for a job. I had a few jobs, none of which
lasted long, before I eventually landed one in the
Albion Motor Works.

That was in the middle of 1910. I remained
there for two and a half years, during which I
acquired much valuable experience. They were a
fine crowd of boys at the Albion and I was quickly
at home among them. I liked the work and
acquired a high degree of proficiency at it. That,
and the fact that I was an excellent time-keeper,
soon made a good impression. But the main thing
was my willingness to help, advise and defend my
mates against any attempted tyranny of the foreman. I soon became the recognised workers' leader
in the factory, acquiring a position of considerable
power and influence. A group quickly collected
around me which was able to keep up a continuous
stream of revolutionary literature, with regular
discussion classes at the midday meal hour.

Outside the factory, at the week-ends and in the
evening, I was continuously engaged in agitation,

giving particular attention to the growing menace of war and conducting anti-militarist propaganda. This brought me an amusing experience in 1912, when I was invited to take the chair at an anti-militarist demonstration organized by the Clarion Scouts in the Pavilion Theatre.

The meeting was to be addressed by Gustave Hervé, a French barrister, the best-known anti-militarist in Europe, soon to become notorious for his gross betrayal of every principle he had ever professed.

Along with Hervé was to speak Guy Bowman, the English Syndicalist who acted as his agent in Britain. Already it was beginning to be obvious that Hervé was preparing to rat, and the Clarion Scouts cancelled his engagement. A frantic search for substitutes was made. At last two were found willing to speak—two Anarchists—Madame Sorge and Guy Aldred.

Madame Sorge was an impressive looking female who affected a huge sombrero hat and a bright red sash around her shoulders. She thought herself the greatest show on earth. She was Napoleon—or thought she was. But Aldred had similar ideas about himself. And how could the lady be Napoleon if the gentleman were really he?

And this was the question that was fought out at the meeting. Instead of being chairman at an anti-imperialist meeting I found myself refereeing at a personality contest between two of the most childish egoists I have ever seen.

I was campaigning closely with John McLean during this period. This brought me into close contact with masses of workers, not only on the Clyde but throughout Scotland as a whole. In Lanarkshire and Fife socialist propaganda was making great headway and already in those early days West Fife was justifying its splendid fighting history, a history which included the winning of the eight-hour day for the miners of Britain.*

But I wasn't campaigning alone, so far as Paisley was concerned. A new Socialist propagandist made his appearance, a pale, sallow-complexioned boy of sixteen or so. His name was John Ross Campbell, and he was a shop assistant employed by the Paisley Co-operative Society. I have never met anyone who so eagerly devoured all the Socialist literature that came his way, nor one who profited so much by what he read. " The Boy," as he was called, started off by taking the chair for me, but very soon he was fully capable of taking the meeting himself.

One incident stands out in my mind in this connection more clearly than any other. It concerns the presence in this country of the deported South African strike leaders. A great protest meeting in their support was held at Paisley, and several of the deportees were present.

* In 1870 when the fight for the shorter working day was being waged in the minefields, the men of West Fife took an historic decision. They decided to cease work at the end of eight hours. This decision they carried out and despite every effort of the owners they stuck to it. It is this great victory which is celebrated at the annual Fife Gala.

We of the S.D.F. had been invited to send a speaker to the meeting, and " The Boy " was chosen as our representative. Two Labour Baillies were the " Top of the Bill." They both did their best to appear statesmanlike, but failed miserably. Then J. R. C. came on. His clear, logical reasoning, coupled with his obvious sincerity, carried the meeting to the highest pitch of enthusiasm. Amidst thunderous applause he sat down and the deportees stepped across the platform and one after another warmly shook him by the hand. We were all very proud of " The Boy."

In the first months of the war he was swept from the grocer's shop into the Army. But throughout the period of his military service I kept up the closest contact with him and when, as a result of wounds and frost-bite he was discharged early in 1918 we took up where we had left off in the early days of the war. He is now one of the best and most loyal comrades in the leadership of the Communist Party.

At the beginning of 1913 I decided to visit America to see two of my sisters who had made their homes in Chicago. Before going I persuaded Jean Roy, who was then and has been ever since my most loyal comrade, to marry me. It is a matter of common knowledge among my comrades that the never-failing support of my wife, her unfailing courage in times of the greatest difficulty and danger, has been one of the most important factors in my life as a revolutionary agitator.

I returned from America in January 1914 and after working for several months in Belfast at steel structural erecting for a Glasgow firm, I got back into the Albion. I received a great welcome from all the boys and by the time the war broke out I had won for myself an established position as the leader of the workers in the factory.

CHAPTER II

IN July 1914 the shop stewards, who were in general the advance guard of Socialism in the factories, went off for their annual summer holidays determined on their return to make the engineering shops 100 per cent trade union in preparation for the struggle that lay ahead in the November of that year. Notice had been given to the employers that, with the termination of the three years' agreement in November, a demand would be made for an increase of twopence per hour. That meant 9s. extra in wages for the 54-hour week, which at that time was the rule, or an increase of weekly rates from 36s. to 45s.

But that 1914 summer was to prove the last carefree holiday for thousands of Clyde workers. Already when we returned to work towards the end of July, the clouds of war were heavy over Europe; and then in the first week in August we were swept into the maelstrom.

What terrible attraction a war can have! The wild excitement, the illusion of wonderful adventure and the actual break in the deadly monotony of working-class life! Thousands went flocking to the colours in the first days, not because of any " love

of country," not because of any high feeling of
" patriotism," but because of the new, strange and
thrilling life that lay before them. Later the reality
of the fearsome slaughterhouse, with all its long
agony of filth and horror, turned them from
buoyant youth to despair or madness.

That the same illusions could be created again was
made evident recently by the Jubilee Celebrations in
London and some provincial centres. Attention
was drawn in the Press to the fact that in the most
poverty-stricken areas the greatest amount of Jubilee
decorations was evident. What a chance in these
unspeakably drab and miserable streets to get some
colour, to get a change, to finish if only for a day or
two with the sordid monotony of life and live free
from police interference and restrictions, as the
" great ones " live! For a little moment, as in the
first days of a war, all barriers are broken down, it
was " their " king as well as that of the dukes and
financiers, exactly in the same sense as it was
" their " country.

But the Clyde was not altogether taken by surprise
when war broke out. Apart from the general
propaganda for Socialism which had for long been
conducted throughout the West of Scotland by
the Social Democratic Party, the Independent
Labour Party and the Socialist Labour Party, there
had been carried on for a number of years an
intense anti-war and anti-militarist propaganda
which continually exposed the war intrigues of the
British Government. In the forefront of this cam-

paign was that indomitable and irrepressible revolutionary fighter, John McLean.

It is not possible for anyone to understand or appreciate the events which took place in Glasgow and the Clyde throughout the years of the war without a knowledge of the part played by this great Scottish revolutionary; yet because of the most wilful and unpardonable neglect, the story of his life, which would have been an inspiration to workers everywhere, has never been published.

When he died, the I.L.P.ers, with whom he had never associated when alive, took an active part in organizing a "Testimonial Fund." For the purposes of this fund, they persuaded Mrs. McLean to hand over to them all McLean's papers and records on the promise that this material would be used for publishing a life of McLean, the proceeds from which would go to the fund. The material was handed over to Maxton. When I heard of this, many months later, I called on Maxton and offered him my assistance. He told me the book was just about finished and that he would let me see it when it was completed.

Since that time I have made several attempts to get the material, as has also J. Figgins of the N.U.R., who was secretary of the McLean Committee, but without avail. The I.L.P. which had no time for McLean when he was alive, has succeeded in suppressing his biography since his death.

John McLean was a schoolmaster, but unlike the group of Glasgow schoolmasters attracted to the

Labour Party and the opportunity for a " brilliant career " by Ramsay MacDonald, McLean became an earnest, energetic disciple of Marx.

His whole life centred in the fight for revolutionary Socialism. Night after night he was on the streets or in the halls. In the summer the long school holidays gave him new opportunities. Everywhere he went he carried the torch. Ayrshire in the West, Dumfries in the South, Fife in the East, Dundee and Aberdeen in the North. All over Scotland he went, rousing the workers for the war against capitalism. Of medium height and sturdy build, he was a living dynamo of energy, driving, always driving towards his goal—the revolutionary struggle for power—the realization of the Socialist Commonwealth.

But he was not only a great mass agitator, masses of workers eagerly crowding to hear him wherever he went; he was above all a great Marxian teacher. His classes, established throughout Scotland, brought crowds of young workers into contact with Marxian Socialism for the first time.

He was the actual founder of the Scottish Labour College, and it would be difficult to travel to any part of the world where the English language is spoken without coming across someone who had been in one of John McLean's classes.

When war was declared his energy and activity surpassed anything we had seen before. From the first moment he declared his Marxian faith—war against the war-makers. Breathing hatred for the capitalist class and the destruction with which it threatened humanity, he went about the streets of Glasgow rousing the workers to a fury of anger against the war and the war-makers. Very soon after the outbreak of war he was arrested, and prosecuted in the police court on a minor charge. This was enough for the school authorities. He was sacked. From that moment all his time was devoted to the fight. Day and night he gave to the cause. He was certainly the greatest revolutionary figure Scotland had produced, and we will meet him again many times later in this book.

Another striking figure, but of an entirely different character, was John Wheatley. Wheatley was a small business man, of miner stock, with a round, pleasant face and a very broad, attractive smile. He wore thick glasses which added to his mild, benevolent appearance, but behind the glasses was a pair of keen, watchful eyes that spoke of a brain ever active and subtle.

He was a Catholic who had outgrown religion. He used to say in a cynical way: " You fellows get terribly excited about God. Why don't you leave Him alone and instead of allowing the others to use religion against you, use it against them? " It was with some such idea that he started the Catholic Socialist Society.

Soon several priests in Glasgow were in full cry against him. He polemized against them to such effect that they started attacking him in the Church. Mob feeling was worked up against him to such an extent that one evening a huge crowd assembled in Shettleston and marched to his house, threatening to stone it and set fire to it. Just as the crowd was approaching the house from one end of the street, the postman arrived at the door from the other. Against the advice of his friends inside, who could hear the roar of the crowd, Wheatley walked to the door, took a letter from the postman, slit it open, and read it calmly on the steps; then, with a casual look at the astonished crowd, he walked in and shut the door. It was as though every one had been drenched with ice-cold water. Not another shout. They scattered ingloriously and disappeared.

That was Wheatley—always able to keep his head, always calm and calculating; but sometimes, when hard pressed, showing the fires of venom that were always banked up.

While there was never open enmity between McLean and Wheatley, there could never be any friendship or collaboration. McLean was utterly uncompromising in his fight for the revolution; Wheatley could see progress only through a continuous series of compromises and intrigues.

But what of the engineers when the war broke out? Wages which had been inadequate before, rapidly became worse. From the very first days the profiteers were on the job. " There's profit in blood "; more, a thousand times more, than in any booze racket in Chicago; and where there are profits the Al Capones of all sizes will be found. Prices first, then rents. The difficulties of the housewives increased daily. In the workshops we agitated continually. Meal-hour discussion circles, with a big sale of revolutionary books, pamphlets and periodicals, had for long been a common feature in most of the Clyde factories, but following the outbreak of war these increased vastly in range and importance.

There is a common illusion that the I.L.P., which was the largest Socialist party numerically in Glasgow and the Clyde area, played a leading role in the fight against war. Nothing could be farther from the truth. The I.L.P. was thoroughly opportunist and, with its traditional adaptability to circumstances, very carefully dodged the issue. About a month after the start of the war the Scottish District of the I.L.P. issued a circular advising I.L.P. propagandists to avoid all controversial questions about the war. It never at any time formulated and carried through a decided policy, but left its members to find their way as best they could, some of them specializing as patriots, while others, especially the younger members, moving towards " Quaker " pacifism.

Typical of the many-sided opportunism of the I.L.P. were P. J. Dollan* and *Forward*, the weekly journal run by Tom Johnston. Dollan, now Glasgow City Treasurer, was at first a " patriot," who " did his bit " in the columns of the *Daily Citizen*,

* When P. J. was in Wakefield gaol in 1917, I was in Leeds fulfilling an engagement and took the opportunity of going to Wakefield. I succeeded in slipping into the prison with a group of C.O. prisoners who were out for the afternoon. The locks had been

until conscription was introduced. That was carrying the war a bit too far, so P. J. developed a conscience. He went to the Home Office scheme at Wakefield, where he spent most of the time in hospital. Later he was allowed a visit to Glasgow on sick leave. He never went back to the scheme.

But while P. J.'s patriotism and pacifism appeared at different stages, *Forward* presented both together. Clever journalistic snippets from the pen of Tom Johnston appeared on the front page, providing revelations about the profiteers, and the sort of people who were fighting for democracy and high ideals, such as the Tsar and some of his Russian, French and British pals; pacifist articles appeared on other pages. But week after week the leading article was filled with the wildest ravings against the Germans. This was the work of Dr. Stirling Robertson, a Glasgow Fabian who wrote under the pen-name of Rob Roy.

While the rank and file of the I.L.P. played their part in the struggles that developed, the party itself was incapable of playing any decisive role in the fight against the war. The most energetic and consistent agitators forming the leadership of the Shop Stewards movement, were a group of S.L.P.ers

---

removed from the cell doors and the prisoners were allowed to freely associate either in the cells or in the hall.

I spent the evening in P. J.'s cell, entertaining a company which included P. J. and Bailie George Smith with selections from Shakespeare and the I.W.W. song book.

who had succeeded in breaking through the paralysing influence of De Leonism.*

Two of these, now dead, were Arthur McManus
and J. W. Muir. The former was physically undersized and not strong, but he had a magnificent head
and a most attractive personality. He was an effective agitator, volatile and witty, and continually in
demand all over the Clyde. " Johnny " Muir was
the complete opposite. He was one of the best
comrades in our movement for preparing and
arguing a case. In less arduous times he would have
been a tower of strength, but his extremely sensitive
nature was quite unfitted for the rough times that
lay ahead. The ordeal of a year's imprisonment in
Calton Jail in 1916 broke his spirit and lost him to
the revolutionary movement.

Of those still alive, Tommy Bell, a hard, never-
tiring worker, stands out. Dour, sometimes to the
point of stubbornness, when defending an opinion,
his apparent harshness and intolerance have often
created the impression of a lack of human sympathy.

But such an impression is entirely wrong. Behind
the rough exterior there is the deepest human feeling
and a wonderful fund of humour. I have been with
him, on what, without his company, would have
been long and tedious journeys. I have been with
him in prison, and participated with him in the
early days of building the party and the Com-

---

* De Leonism, called after Daniel De Leon, an American Socialist,
the founder of the Socialist Labour Party, which spread from
U.S.A. to Scotland, but is now virtually extinct in both countries.

munist International and always he was the loyal, dependable comrade, who stood strong and firm no matter how the tide might flow against him.

Then there was Tommy Clark, Glasgow's greatest declaimer of De Leon's petty bourgeois phantasies. At one time, Tommy aspired to be known as a sort of trade union iconoclast, a terror to the bureaucrats; but now alas, he sits at the headquarters of the Amalgamated Engineering Union in Peckham Road, surrounded by icons in the form of rules and regulations, and woe betide the unhappy mortal who fails to bow down to them. Supported by the militants, he got elected to the A.E.U. Executive, since when he has moved farther and farther away from his former associations.

Another outstanding figure was David Kirkwood, who finished with the S.L.P. early in the war. Johnny Muir, who was editor of the *Socialist*, the S.L.P. organ, was trying to argue a case for a Socialist defending " his own " country, at a special meeting in their hall in Renfrew Street. In the midst of the discussion, and while Johnny was arguing a certain point, Davy jumped up and shouted, " Naw, naw, Joanie, that'll no dae, the workers have nae country. Ah'm feenished wi' ye." He shook the dirt of Renfrew Street from his feet and found a new haven and ultimately an empire in the I.L.P.

For myself, I was a member of the B.S.P., and at that time a disciple of John McLean. The B.S.P. was supposed to be a Marxist organization, but it was dominated by the top-hatted Hyndman, who had a special Marxist brand of his own.

For many years a fight for genuine Marxism had been carried on by McLean against the Hyndman group, but this question was resolved by the war. Hyndman was an imperialist and came out in support of the war. This led to a split in the party: the minority, with Hyndman, formed the patriotic National Socialist Party, the majority carried on the party with a definite anti-war policy.

I was already well-known as a revolutionary agitator, and although I was on fairly good terms with the I.L.P. in Glasgow, I never missed an opportunity of exposing the opportunism of the I.L.P. leaders. On one occasion, several years before the war, while speaking at a meeting in Clydebank, I referred to MacDonald as the " Pecksniff " and Snowden as the " Uriah Heep " of the Socialist Movement. This caused considerable anger in I.L.P. and Labour Party circles. After the first Labour Government in 1924, a woman spoke to me after a meeting in the City Hall, Glasgow. She reminded me of that earlier meeting and of what I had said, and told me she had been very angry, calling me every name she could think of. " Now," she added, " I recognize you were quite right."

On the first Sunday of the war, while John McLean was rousing Glasgow, I, with the help of a few comrades, organized a mass demonstration in my home town, Paisley. I went all out against the war and against the young fellows joining up. There were a few uneasy " patriots " in the crowd, but on the whole the meeting favoured the line I was advocating. This was brought out more clearly a few weeks later when, at one of our regular Sunday meetings, I was challenged to a debate. The challenger was a " patriotic " Socialist, who lived in Renfrew, a town three miles from Paisley.

When the debate took place he served up the usual stuff about Germany being the aggressor and how necessary it was for the salvation of mankind that German militarism should be destroyed.

" I have a dark road to travel home," he said. " If someone on that road attacks me with a big club, I want to ask Mr. Gallacher if I would be justified in using a big club to defend myself? "

I showed how all the countries had been preparing for war for years; how the whole of British diplomacy had been directed towards isolating Britain's great trade rival, Germany; how Edward the Seventh, called the Peacemaker, had really been the " Pacemaker " for war, and that what we had to destroy was capitalism, beginning in our own country. As for the " big club," I said: " If anybody attacks you with a big club, I've no objection to you using a big club, or even two if you can handle them. And if Bethman Hollweg uses a big club to attack Sir Edward Grey, I've no objection to Sir Edward Grey using a big club on Bethman Hollweg; but one thing I'm damned sure of, I'm not going to be the big club and I'm going to do all I can to prevent the working class being used as the

big club. We are accustomed to hear Irish National-
ists declare that ' England's adversity is Ireland's
opportunity; ' I'll paraphrase that and say the
adversity of the capitalist class is the opportunity of
the working class. Let us take advantage of it and
go forward for a victory, not for the imperialist
allies, but for the working class."

When my opponent got up the second time he
gave himself away completely. He appealed to the
young men to volunteer for service. " If you don't,"
he cried, " conscription will be introduced and those
of us who are married will have to go." The crowd
laughed him off the platform. He never showed up
any more.

But it was not only on Sunday nights that
meetings were held. Far from it. Every night in
the week was utilized for anti-war propaganda.
With John McLean leading, every available agitator
was brought on to the job. Rents, prices, wages,
wholesale slaughter—and for what? The famous
Kitchener poster affirmed that " Your King and
Country need you," but wherever you read this
you could also read:

> " Your King and Country Need You,
>   Ye hardy sons of toil.
> But will your King and Country need you
>   When they're sharing out the spoil? "

Already in the earliest days we could show that
every " racketeer," big and little, was on the job;
that the slaughter was going on not in the interests

of the workers but in order to suppress working-class rights and intensify exploitation. Great support was gained in all parts of the Clyde, but the majority of the workers, so long under the influence of the Yellow Press, still hung in the balance. It needed the fight on the wage issue to open their eyes and show them what was actually going on.

CHAPTER III

BY November the campaign against the war, against high prices and rents and for increased wages was in full blast. Housewives as well as factory workers were being brought into political activity. The Clyde area was beginning to wake up —but only beginning.

And in November negotiations with the employers were begun on the tuppence-an-hour increase. I was an executive member of the United Brassfounders' Association, one of the smaller unions which, with some others, amalgamated with the Amalgamated Society of Engineers after the war, forming the Amalgamated Engineering Union.

As an executive member of my union I was elected to the Allied Trades Committee, which conducted negotiations with the employers on behalf of the Boilermakers, Joiners, Pattern-makers, " Brassies," General Labourers and several other sections. Another committee, composed of the A.S.E., Plumbers and two or three other unions, carried on separate negotiations with the same employers for the same demand. The negotiations were scandalous and provided new fuel for setting the Clyde ablaze. I reported all that happened to

32

the shop stewards and thus it reached the factories and branch meetings.

The employers offered each committee an increase of a halfpenny per hour, and then, after long discussions with the Engineering Committee, raised the offer to three farthings. Our Committee then had another go at it, and we got the three farthings offer. This was followed by more discussion with the Engineeering Committe—then a deadlock. Then a suggestion was put forward in our committee (the Allied Trades), that we should try to induce the employers to spring another farthing and settle with them for a penny an hour increase. Thus the smaller unions were to be used to " double-cross " the A.S.E. and at the same time betray the fight of the workers for the tuppence an hour.

I launched a violent attack on the originator of this proposal, Bailie Whitehead, the secretary of a small West of Scotland brassworkers' union. Most of those on the committee were prominent officials, and it was obvious that they sympathized with the proposal, although they were careful not to commit themselves openly. But it was clear that if the employers offered a penny they would jump at it. I was still working in the Albion Motor Works and they tried every dodge to keep me from attending the meetings. They even went so far on one occasion as to close the meeting, disperse, and then by a prearrangement meet again without my knowledge. But my suspicions had been aroused, and when one of my colleagues left me with a mumbled excuse and I noticed he was going back the way we had just come, I decided to follow him and, to the consternation of the committee, came breezing in just when they had all got comfortably seated.

As we were to meet the employers the following day, this manœuvre had been carried out so that they could go ahead with an agreed policy of " a penny and we'll settle." My appearance upset their little plan. We met the employers next day with our original demand and no agreement on anything else. But the employers were adamant and would not advance on the three farthings. It was clear to them that our side was not prepared to make a fight and all they had to do was sit tight and talk " patriotic."

One of them, representing a Paisley firm, let himself go on the " plight of the boys in the trenches," and how it was the duty of all of us to work and work and see that they had everything required for victory. Our side chipped in with " hear-hears " and gave full approval to his patriotic zeal. Then I told him and the others that he had a damned cheek to talk to us in such a manner. I said: " You're not concerned about the ' boys in the trenches '; they can be blown to hell for all you care. It's profit you're after! There are two big guns at Greenlaw Goods Station; they've been lying there for three weeks and your firm refuses to touch them till the price is raised fifty per cent. Will you go out and tell the ' boys in the trenches ' that? All right," I continued, " I'll tell you something. We're concerned about the ' boys in the factories.' We want twopence an hour and we're prepared to fight to get it."

There was a general hubbub when I finished. The employers were indignant, whispering to one another and obviously preparing to break off negotiations. Thomson, the Blacksmiths' official, muttered to some of the others, " For Christ's sake, get him out of here, he'll spoil everything." But he was too late. The " spoiling " had been done. The employers proposed to adjourn the meeting, so there was nothing left to do but to retire and lick our sores.

What a time we had then! Whitehead, Thomson and several others were wild. Whitehead maintained that the employers were on the point of conceding the other farthing until I intervened.

" We can't carry on negotiations with this man present," he declared, " the employers won't meet us any more if we have him with us."

" Well," I replied, " you may not be able to carry on negotiations with me, but you're going to have a hard job negotiating without me. For where you are there will I be also." The significant thing about this meeting, however, was the fact that Whitehead and Thomson were left with a very small minority. The majority of the officials supported the line I had taken and strongly opposed any further attempts to settle apart from the A.S.E., which was insisting on the full demand.

November and December passed, and we were

now in January 1915. Towards the end of January a meeting of members was called by the Brass-founders' Association in the St. Mungo Hall. The hall was packed, everybody being in fighting mood. The general secretary of the society, John Jeffers, had come up from Manchester. I made a speech in which I outlined the character of the negotiations and the cynical attitude of the employers. " They think we're afraid to take action," I said, " and the conduct of some of the officials has certainly encouraged that idea. They think that because there are two committees negotiating, the forces are split. We must show them different. We must declare our solidarity with the A.S.E. in the fight for the full demand. We must declare our readiness to take whatever action the circumstances demand."

John Jeffers made a cautious speech in which he expressed the hope that nothing rash would be done; at the same time he stated that the union was behind the men in the fight for the tuppence-an-hour increase.

One of the members asked what our Glasgow organizer had been doing during the discussions on the Allied Trades Committee and in the negotiations with the employers. " Is he a dummy ? " The organizer jumped to his feet: " No, I'm not a dummy," he declared, " I supported Gallacher in everything he said." This meeting unanimously declared for solidarity with the A.S.E. and for action to secure the full demand.

As will be readily understood, the issue was now the subject of everyday discussion in the factories and union branches. By far the most powerful union was the A.S.E. Its district secretary, Sam Buntin, and district organizer, Brodie, were anxious to get a settlement and would have made big concessions to secure it. But the membership, the branches and the District Committee were strong for the full demand. If Whitehead and company had succeeded in pulling off a settlement at a penny an hour, then of course Brodie and Buntin could have used this as a reason for settling on the same terms for the engineers. Nothing could have been better for weakening the opposition of the engineers than the ability to point out that all the other unions represented in the Allied Trades had given up the fight and accepted a settlement. But now the majority of these unions, through their official representatives, had declared themselves not for a separate settlement, but for solidarity behind the engineers. This strengthened the whole character of the struggle and the agitation around it.

John McLean, through his Marxist classes, was supplying a continuous stream of material for the agitation. McLean never dealt in " abstract " Marxism of the Kautsky variety. He applied his Marxist knowledge to the events around him and used all that was happening to show the truth of Marxism. He demonstrated in the clearest manner that the war was a war for trade and brought out into full relief the sinister robber forces behind it.

He gave example after example of the financiers and big employers pointing a gun at the head of the Government and demanding increased profits, and of other firms selling war material to neutrals with the full knowledge that they were being re-sold to Germany.

These examples, with instances of increased prices for ordinary commodities and higher rents, were carried day after day into the factories. " The boys at the front " were being slaughtered for profit, and the very slaughter of the workers at the front was being used for increased robbery of the workers at home. War against the employers, against the " profiteers," against the " rent-rackers " was now beginning to overshadow the " war against Germany " in the minds of the Clyde workers.

Then, early in February, while the employers were still adamant in their refusal to grant the tuppence increase, a new " incident " occurred, and the whole Clyde area was brought into action. As a consequence of the rush of recruits in the early days of the war and the great demand for output with which the factories were faced, there was an actual shortage of skilled workers for the engineering shops.

Weir's, of Cathcart, which specialized in air-feed and discharge pumps for the Admiralty, had a large body of engineers, turners and fitters of a very high quality. But Weir's were short of men, so they engaged some in America. They gave them a return ticket from America to Britain, 10s. more a week than their own men were getting—although these latter, because of their experience in this particular class of work, were far ahead of the Americans—and a guaranteed bonus of £10 at the end of six months besides the higher wages. The consequences of such an action might have been foreseen. But, because of the " patriotic " posturings of the national trade union officials, who were vying with each other in declarations of servility to the war-mongers, and the weakness of some of the district officials, the employers were convinced that there was no possibility of the workers taking action. They were prepared to put across the rawest kind of deal.

But while the national officials of the trade union movement were truckling to the Government and " agreeing " that trade union rights should be " suspended," while they were, in fact, being parties to the crime of weakening the trade unions at a time when it was more than ever necessary that they should be strong, the workers in Cathcart faced the question quite otherwise. For the very life of trade unionism was at stake. If the employers had got away with what they tried at Cathcart, trade unionism in this country would have received its heaviest blow, one from which it would not have recovered easily. Whatever else happened at that period, one thing is sure: the engineers at Cathcart, by their prompt action in declaring a strike when faced with such a situation, maintained in the face of all the betrayals of the national officials the right of the unions to determine the conditions to be operated in the factories. They demonstrated to the Government and the employers that, war or no war, the workers were going to see that the trades unions did not go out of existence, but would have to be reckoned with as the fighting organs of the working class.

.   .   .   .   .

Weir's was one of the best organized shops in Glasgow, with a fine body of shop stewards, all of whom had been taking the keenest interest in the discussions with the employers.

On Tuesday, February 16, following the introduction of the higher paid Americans, the shop stewards called a meeting and a decision was taken for immediate strike action. The following morning a mass meeting of the strikers was held in the St. Mungo Hall, where a decision calling on the other shops for supporting action was expected. But before the meeting came together, the movement was already spreading. The morning following the decision to strike we had a consultation of shop stewards in the Albion Motor Works, where I was employed. We decided for action with Weir's and as a consequence called a mass meeting for 9 a.m., the breakfast meal-hour. The meeting unanimously supported the proposal for a stoppage and a delegation was appointed to attend Weir's meeting at St. Mungo Hall, with a declaration of solidarity. We also got into touch with Yarrow's and Meechan's to ensure that they also took action.

When the delegation from the Albion, of which I was the leader, arrived at St. Mungo Hall, we witnessed a strange sight. The hall was packed with strikers, tense because of the very circumstances of the strike. On the platform addressing them was a small insignificant figure, obviously very perturbed at the situation in which he found himself. This was Councillor George Kerr, who, with one or two of his Labour colleagues, had been invited to speak at the meeting and had come without being actually alive to what was going on.

The worthy Councillor was talking about housing and how important it was to vote Labour at the Municipal Elections in November. There was muttering all over the hall as our delegation passed through to the platform room. Tommy Clark came forward with his hand out, " Thank Christ, you're here," he said; " this fellow " (meaning Councillor Kerr) " will start a riot."

I was introduced to several shop stewards whom I hadn't met before, one of whom, J. M. Messer, became afterwards secretary of the Clyde Workers' Committee. I was then taken to the platform. The Councillor finished his house-building and hurried off.

I said that I brought greetings from the Albion and a pledge of solidarity so long as the fight lasted. I told them Yarrow's and Meechan's were on the move and that before the day was out we would have the whole of Clydeside closed down. What a scene there was as they jumped to their feet and cheered! That morning they had been alone, now all the others were marching into line. What an inspiration it was to them. And what an inspiration they were to the other delegates now arriving from the other factories, at the hall. It was as I had said. By the evening all the principal factories had decided. The great Clyde Strike of February 1915 was on.

The strike was, and still is, wrongly referred to as an " unofficial " strike. Such a term is entirely misleading. Branch officials, district officials and in some cases, executive officials (like myself) were involved. The more correct term for such a strike is " spontaneous strike." Such strikes have played an important part in the development of the trade union movement and are often recognized and supported by the national officials. Such a strike is necessary when something occurs, leaving only the option of submitting or fighting. It may be the introduction of a non-unionist, where trade union membership is insisted on by the union as a condition of employment. It may be a cut in a recognized rate or, as was the case at Weir's, the introduction of privileged workers from outside at the expense of Weir's own employees.

If ever there was a " spontaneous " strike that called for the support of the national officials, this was the one. We had no objection to American engineers or any others getting jobs ; we had no objection to their getting high wages, but we certainly did object, as trade unionists ought to object, to working ourselves at the same job for lower wages.

At the St. Mungo Hall meeting we decided to hold mass meetings in all the areas round the principal factories the following morning and to send in the afternoon a representative from each area to a meeting at which a Central Strike Committee would be formed.

These mass meetings were tremendous and gave everyone a great feeling of power. The representatives met in the afternoon at the Herald League Bookshop, George Street, which was run by an old comrade, W. McGill, and his wife, and was the headquarters of a semi-anarchist group associated with the *Weekly Herald*.

In order to escape the threats of the Defence of the Realm Act, we formed, instead of a " Strike " Committee, a " Labour-Withholding " Committee, with myself as chairman and J. M. Messer as secretary. At our first meeting we had to take note of the fact that the Government had hurriedly called together the national officials of the bigger unions and had given them their instructions— " Call off this strike."

Representatives of the national committees rushed to Glasgow and did their utmost to break the strike. But they got a rough reception. What a spectacle they presented! Not an argument of any kind against the strike; intimidated by the Government, they were merely maudlin in their pleading to us to give it up.

An old friend of mine, who had gone to work with me for many years, and had later been elected

from the area to the A.S.E. executive, said to some
of us: " It's all right for you fellows, but we've
been called up by the Government and, while they
were very suave and courteous, we could feel the
threat behind all they said."

" What threat ? " we asked.

" The threat of imprisonment," he replied.

" Who for ? "

" For us," he moaned.

Did we laugh! We were like the absentee Irish
landlord who refused to be intimidated by threats
against the life of his bailiff. Old " Sanny " got no
sympathy from us.

The *Glasgow Herald* of Friday, February 19,
reported a meeting at the Palace Theatre, in the
south side of Glasgow, at which Brownlie, Gorman
and Burton, from the Executive Committee of the
A.S.E. were present. The report reads as follows:

" The men were very adverse in their criticism of the
Executive Council and interrupted Mr. Brownlie a good
deal when he attempted to persuade them to act on the
advice of their council and resume work. One of the
other Council members they declined to hear. In the end
they passed a unanimous resolution in favour of remaining
idle until the advance of 2d. per hour was granted."

But I do not think it would be possible now to
get anything like an understanding of the atmosphere which surrounded this great strike. All over
the country the Press, platform and pulpit had
been used to whip up a frenzy of hate. War-fever

was spreading like an evil plague. Atrocity stories and propaganda lies of every kind were being served out and eagerly taken up. Anyone who dared to raise his voice in protest was a " pro-German," if not an actual hired agent of the enemy. Into the midst of all this madness, all these lies and hypocrisy, burst the strike on the Clyde. What a roar of rage went up from the war-makers! The Press shrieked for action against the leaders; everywhere in the ranks of the bourgeoisie and petty-bourgeoisie we were cursed and condemned. Of all the multitude of Press organs, with the exception of one or two weeklies with very small circulations, there was not one to say a word for us. *Forward* remained discreetly silent. Dollan poured his daily dose of " patriotism " into the *Daily Citizen.*

When two weeks later the time came to call off the strike, a group of journalists was waiting outside the bookshop for our decision. Amongst them was Dollan. Tommy Clark and the others asked me to try to persuade him to come in. I went out and used all my persuasive powers. I told him we wanted to give him the first information. It was no use. P.J. knew that what was waiting for him was not news, and decided to remain in the vicinity of his fellow-journalists.

Travelling around the area in tram or train you could hear the strike discussed. Shopkeepers and small business men were venomous. " The leaders should be shot." " It's obvious they're in the pay

of the Germans." " This man McLean is the cause
of all the trouble; why don't they lock him up? "
These and similar remarks could be heard everywhere, as well as references to the personal appearance and character of the strike leaders. But what
I could never understand was the fact that no matter
what might be said about the others, one thing was
always said about me—in tram and train I heard it
dozens of times. Some little shopkeepers going from
Glasgow to Bridge-of-Weir or thereabouts would
get talking in a railway carriage. The strike was
condemned, McLean was condemned, some of the
others would get their turn, and then—" This
Gallacher, I understand he's just a drunken black-
guard." How such a rabid prohibitionist as I was
should always be referred to in such a way was a
mystery to me. As day followed day and the strike
continued, the attacks on us became terrific.

Before the strike began the A.S.E. in the West
of Scotland area had decided to take a ballot of the
members on the employers' offer of three farthings
per hour. A few days after the strike broke out
the figures were published as follows:

	For	Against
Glasgow	504	6,439
Dumbarton	23	310
Greenock	91	693
Paisley	160	988
Mid Lanark	37	356
North Ayrshire	14	140
	829	8,926

Yet, despite this vote, the A.S.E. officials did everything to break the strike. Failing in other directions they tried to penetrate the ranks in an exceptionally despicable way. While the committee as a whole represented the A.S.E., I, as chairman, was not in that union but in the United Brass-founders. Insidious suggestions were made about the " brassies " being out to injure the A.S.E. and the strike being used by me for that purpose. Of course I knew this was not likely to have any serious effect, but at the same time I knew that in such a critical situation everything, no matter how small, counted, and so I insisted that an A.S.E. man should figure as the chairman. Tommy Clark vigorously opposed this and declared that nobody would pay any attention to this latest effort at disruption, but I succeeded in persuading them to make the change, although it was only formal and did not affect in any way the conduct of the strike.

Every morning mass meetings were held in the areas and the discussions and decisions of the previous day's committee meeting were reported. Every afternoon and evening the committee was in session, taking reports from the areas and considering ways and means of strengthening and extending the strike. For a fortnight, under the most terrific barrage ever directed against a strike, we kept going without a break of any kind, despite the fact that not one striker was receiving a penny of strike pay or relief. But we knew we couldn't carry on much longer without a measure of disintegration setting in, and that we wanted to avoid at all cost.

So we made preparations to call off the strike. We went to the area meetings and reported our view of the situation and the importance of all going back as we came out, organized and strong. From every meeting we got a resolution of confidence in the committee and a pledge of support for whatever steps we decided to take. The night we called it off the meeting place, as I mentioned before, was besieged by reporters, all eagerly awaiting our decision. Inside we had a very serious discussion, after which I drew up a short resolution embodying our decisions. This resolution recognized the magnificent response made by the workers all over the Clyde and the determination of all to maintain the fight for the full increase. But in the circumstances confronting us it was impossible to continue the strike any longer, and we called on the workers to return as they had come out—as one man. So far the resolution was good news to the enemy and his Press, but the conclusion of the resolution sent them into an even more violent paroxysm than the original strike-call itself. " The strike continues," the resolution ended, " but now inside the factories. We call on all workers to operate a ' stay-in ' strike." Ca' canny was the order of the day.

It was a great strike. The loyalty and solidarity of the workers could not have been higher. The organization and contacts between the factories and the areas and between the areas and the centre was almost perfect. It ended, not on a note of defeat, but with a feeling of something achieved—the workers of the Clyde had broken through the rotten atmosphere of war-jingoism and stood out, strong and unafraid, ready to defend their class against their class enemies.

Commenting on the strike, the *Herald* of March 20, said:

" The Labour-Withholding Committee can congratulate itself on having fought well. It can be sure that in the near future its efforts will again have to be exerted. Despite insults and threats, despite official pressure, the Clyde men have kept the flag of revolutionary trade unionism flying and that itself is something."

Later, in dealing with the fact that the Liberal Government was now being faced with a rising stream of opposition, the *Herald* remarks: " If one asks what event disillusioned the Liberal syndicate " (Government—W. G.) "the answer is the Clyde dispute—that and nothing else."

CHAPTER IV

"WE ARE NOT PAYING INCREASED RENT"

THE strike was over. We were back once more in the factories. But the strike had made a deep political change. Any hope the war-makers might have had of spreading the war fever throughout the Clyde was now gone for ever. The workers knew their enemies, and that they were not across the North Sea. Revolutionary agitators, under McLean's tuition, were increasing in number day by day, and were warmly cheered at mass meetings wherever they went. It became increasingly difficult for the " patriots " to get a hearing. From the very beginning the Socialists of Glasgow took a firm stand against the war. This was evidenced when Ben Tillet, the first of the big " Defend our Country " demagogues to visit Glasgow, came to fulfil an engagement with the Clarion Scouts. The meeting was in the Pavilion Theatre, which for many years had been used by the Clarion Scouts for winter lectures.

Ben, who from the " back of the Front " shrieked his undying hatred of the Hun and proclaimed his intention to return to Britain to preach " bloody murder," tried to put across " defence of our country," " our noble war aims," and the rest of it,

50

but the audience of Socialists hooted him off the platform.

Now, following the strike, the great mass of the workers were prepared to give the same short shrift to the " patriots " ; in every factory literature distribution and discussion were going on with greater intensity than ever. And what was of first-class importance for the development of the struggle in all the principal factories, workshop committees representing all departments and all workers were now functioning.

These were a direct outcome of the strike. While certain of the unions had always had shop stewards functioning more or less actively, these in the main were only concerned with their own members and quite often many departments or many sections of workers had no shop stewards at all. But with the strike, as each factory came out, a committee was elected with representatives from each department or section. The Strike Committee represented and covered every worker in the factory and on return to work, remained as a Works Committee, responsible for the complete organization of the factory. The Central Labour-Withholding Committee also kept together, meeting regularly to discuss the situation and to take what steps were possible to advance the struggle for wages and for the protection of trade union rights.

With the passing of the Munitions Act, made possible by the collaboration of the trade union leaders with Lloyd George, daily problems arose and the need for a permanent organization became evident. Out of the Labour-Withholding Committee, therefore, the Clyde Workers' Committee was born. I was elected chairman and J. M. Messer, secretary; one of our first acts was to issue a leaflet on the character of the struggle before us. A passage in the leaflet, heavily underlined, read:

" The support given to the Government by the Trade Union leaders is an act of grossest treachery to the working class."

The leaflet was signed by myself and Messer, as chairman and secretary of the commitee.

At the subsequent Trade Union Congress, Arthur Henderson appeared in all his glory as a member of the Government, and, waving the leaflet above his head, demanded action against the signatories. Alas for Arthur! While many of the officials present would willingly have obliged, they were not in a position to do so. Expulsions on the Clyde at that moment would have been disastrous—for those who ordered them.

During the whole period of the strike, the campaign against increased rents had been growing in volume. Following the strike, greater forces than ever were thrown into it. In Govan, Mrs. Barbour, a typical working-class housewife, became the leader of a movement such as had never been seen before, or since for that matter. Street meetings, back-court meetings, drums, bells, trumpets—every method was used to bring the women out and organize them for the struggle. Notices were printed by the thousand and put up in the windows: wherever you went you could see them. In street after street, scarcely a window without one: " WE ARE NOT PAYING INCREASED RENT."

These notices represented a spirit amongst the women that could not be overcome. The factors (agents for the property owners) could not collect the rents. They applied to the courts for eviction warrants. Having obtained these, sheriff's officers were sent to serve them and evict the tenants. But Mrs. Barbour had a team of women who were wonderful. They could smell a sheriff's officer a mile away. At their summons women left their cooking, washing or whatever they were doing. Before they got anywhere near their destination, the officer and his men would be met by an army of furious women who drove them back in a hurried scramble for safety.

Attempt after attempt was made to secure evictions, all of which ended in futility. The increased rent could not be collected, the tenants could not be evicted. Then some legal genius had a brainwave. The property owners and factors sat back and laughed as they thought of it. It was so simple and so effective. Why hadn't they thought of it before? Mrs. Barbour and her army of women were a terror to them no longer. They simply walked over their heads and sued the householder at the " small debt " court. By this means workers were summoned to attend the court and show reason why

their wages should not be impounded to liquidate
the debt claimed by the factor in the form of rent.
In such a case the factor could not only get a
decision allowing him to get his rent from the
employer out of the wages of the worker, but he
could also ask for a judgment placing the costs
of the proceedings as an extra burden on the
tenants.

After a few such cases, with the workers affected
coming home with only half their wages, the others
would rapidly have become demoralized and the
resistance to increased rent would be finished.
This, at any rate, was how the factors reasoned.
It was a great idea and it was sure to work. So
summonses were sought and issued to a group of
tenants employed in the yards. But they had
reckoned without Mrs. Barbour and the Clyde shop
stewards.

" Will we let them get away with this ? " was the
new war-cry resounding in every street. " Never! "
thundered the reply from the women. All day
long, in the streets, in the halls, in the houses,
meetings were held. Kitchen meetings, street
meetings, mass meetings, meetings of every kind.
No halt, no rest for anyone, all in preparation for
the sitting of the court when the test case came on.
As in the streets, so in the factories. " Will we allow
the factors to attack our wages ? " " Never! "
Every factory was keyed up and ready.

On the day of the trial Glasgow witnessed a
demonstration the like of which had never been

seen before. From early morning the women were marching to the centre of the city where the sheriff's court is situated. Mrs. Barbour's army was on the march. But even as they marched, mighty reinforcements were coming from the workshops and the yards. From far away Dalmuir in the West, from Parkhead in the East, from Cathcart in the South and Hydepark in the North, the dungareed army of the proletariat invaded the centre of the city.

At the Albion we formed up at breakfast-time and were joined by Yarrow's and Meechan's. In the main road we awaited the arrival of the contingents from Dalmuir* and Clydebank. Then on we went, leaving the factories empty and deserted, shouting and singing.

As we marched along Argyle Street near the Central Station, we passed a section of another army moving in the opposite direction, on the way to France. Some of the young chaps gave us a cheer as we passed, but many others looked pathetically towards us as our fellows shouted " Down tools, boys! " and gave the impression that very little persuasion would have brought them over into our ranks.

Into the streets around the Sheriff's Court the workers marched from all sides. All the streets were packed. Traffic was completely stopped.

---

* Dalmuir, where several of the men were employed, had sent on a deputation to the Court to inform the Sheriff that if there was a conviction, they would immediately declare a strike.

Right in front of the court, John McLean was on a platform addressing the crowd as far as his voice could reach. In other streets near the court others of us were at it. Our platforms were unique. Long poster-boards had been picked up from the front of newspaper shops. These were placed on the shoulders of half a dozen husky, well-matched workers and the speaker was lifted on to them. It was a great experience, speaking from a yielding platform and keeping a measure of balance while flaying the factors and the war-makers. Roar after roar of rage went up as incidents were related showing the robbery of mothers and wives whose sons and husbands were at the front. Roar followed roar as we pictured what would happen if we allowed the attack on our wages.

It was put very popularly in the following form: " What did you do in the Great War, Daddy ? " asked the boy whose father was an engineer. (This question, by the way, was then to be seen on all recruiting posters and was intended to shame men into the army.) " I did munition work, my boy," the father answered. " What did you do in the Great War, Daddy ? " asked the boy who was the son of a factor. " My boy," answered the factor, " I *did* munition workers."

Inside the court the sheriff and his clerks were white with apprehension. A deputation of workers, men and women, was demanding to be heard. The roars from outside were making the windows rattle. At any moment the deputation might be followed

by a surging, irresistible crowd of angry men and
women. In such circumstances how was it possible
for a poor sheriff to retain any dignity—how was it
possible to make play with legal technicalities and
trivialities? There was no hope of the police doing
anything. They were helpless, and what use is a
court, what power has a judge, apart from the brute
force they are able to employ?

It was obvious to the sheriff that the situation was
too desperate to play with. He telephoned to
London and got put through to the Minister of
Munitions, Mr. Lloyd George. " The workers have
left the factories," he said, after explaining the
character of the case. " They are threatening to
pull down Glasgow. What am I to do? " " Stop
the case," he was told, "a Rent Restriction Act will
be introduced immediately."

When this news was relayed there was a scene of
enthusiasm that baffles description. Shouting, singing, cheering, the great demonstration started to
move again. All night long the celebration of
victory went on. The " great idea " of the factors
had been blown sky-high through the determination of the women and the solidarity and organization of the workers on the Clyde and in this way
the Rent Restriction Act was won for the workers
of the country.

The *Herald* offered this tribute to the men and
women of the Clyde: " Thanks to the fine stand
made by the Glasgow women and the determined
attitude of the Clyde munition workers, the Govern-

ment has introduced a Bill to legalize pre-war rent during the war and for six months thereafter."

But while the Rent Restriction Act was a victory, the Munitions Act was a continual menace. Day after day attempts were made to encroach on the conditions and practices operating in the workshops, which only the strength of our organization prevented. "Munition" courts had been set up, but these we turned into a farce. Always when a "case" was on the court was crowded with demonstrating workers, with McGill of the Herald League moving among the seats, shouting his periodicals and pamphlets. All the time the movement was growing in strength in the factories and at the centre. Some of us in the factories, as chairmen of the factory committees, held positions of extraordinary power, quite immune from any interference from the management.

Every Saturday afternoon the delegates from the factories met in a hall in Ingram Street. From 250 to 300 was the usual number of delegates present, with all the principal undertakings represented. While I, a member of the B.S.P., occupied the chair, with J. M. Messer, a member of the I.L.P., as secretary, practically all the other members of the small leading committee, which met two nights a week, were members of the S.L.P., which had broken away from the impossible doctrinaires of De Leon. One or other of these, therefore, would report for the leading committee on organization or policy.

At the general delegate meeting we had warmly

welcomed John McLean and J. D. McDougall, a young bank clerk, who was then playing a big part as a lecturer in McLean's classes and was generally looked upon as his first lieutenant. Both were allowed full right to participate in all discussions and on many occasions were helpful and encouraging. Then, suddenly, we were favoured with a new visitor, and with his coming, trouble soon started.

This was a fellow named Peter Petrov. I had already met him in 1912 in Manchester. I was there attending the first conference of the B.S.P., following its formation from the S.D.P., and some other scattered elements. At this conference there was a big drive against Hyndman and his policy, in which I took a leading part. At lunch-time on the second day of the conference I went away on my own to have a quiet snack (I had been in a very heated scene before the adjournment). As I walked along the street, I heard a voice say in a hissing whisper, "Comrade Gallacher!" I turned round and faced the revolutionary of melodrama. A sharp, dark face with black restless eyes, hooked nose, small dark moustache covering a short upper lip, which, continually receding from a set of white gleaming teeth, gave the impression of a perpetual grin.

He told me his name was Petrov; he was a great Marxist, he was writing a great book on Marxism; he told me a whole host of things, and then he started telling me things about Hyndman, about

Quelch, about Rothstein and everybody else of note in the B.S.P. The more he talked the more irresponsible became his accusations, and the more pronounced was the grin. He completely ruined my snack and when at the conclusion of it all, he expressed the hope that he would see a lot of me, I said things to myself. I succeeded in dodging him the rest of the time; he never got another chance at me.

Now, here he was in Glasgow, the hot-bed of the proletarian struggle in the middle of 1915. He attached himself to John McLean, and John brought him along to the delegate meeting of the Clyde Workers' Committee. He introduced him and asked us to receive him as a fraternal delegate, which we did, following which Petrov said a few words of appreciation. We accepted him in good faith. But he played havoc with McLean and McDougall. Nothing but whispering. Something about this one, something about the other. Soon McLean and McDougall were suspicious of everybody. At the delegate meetings they began to throw out hints about certain of the leaders, with Petrov's white-toothed grin and nodding head supplying the encouragement. It was quite obvious that something had to be done or serious disruption would follow.

Then, one Saturday, Johnny Muir gave a lengthy report on the campaign we were preparing in connection with " dilution of labour," which was then being discussed. An elaboration of this report was presented by the same comrade when Lloyd George made his historic visit to the Clyde. But no sooner had he finished on this occasion than up jumped Petrov. With a small group of delegates, amongst whom was McDougall, cheering him on (McLean was not present at the moment) he launched an almost incredible attack on Johnny Muir and the other members of the S.L.P. who were in the leadership of the movement.

We were all so taken by surprise, we could only look at one another and gasp. As chairman, I called Petrov to order and after some difficulty got him to resume his seat. I then said that in view of what had been going on for some time, we could not view such an outrageous attack as he had made on Johnny Muir other than as a deliberate attempt to disrupt the committee; therefore I would take a proposal from the meeting that Petrov be not allowed to attend any further meetings. At this, McDougall jumped up in a passion and declared that I was taking advantage of a foreigner. " It's an example of race hatred," he shouted.

" All right," I replied, " just to show there isn't anything racial about it I'll ask the delegates to add your name to the proposal."

The motion was put and with the exception of the small group of half a dozen closely associated with McDougall, the voting was unanimous. When the meeting concluded they were waiting for me at the door. McDougall and McLean, who had arrived late, and I, got into quite a heated argument.

Petrov, with the grin working overtime, kept up a continual chorus of three words, " Gallacher, you pig." That ended his attempt to disrupt the Clyde Workers' Committee, but not, alas, his influence on McDougall and McLean.

During this period two cases of workers being imprisoned occurred, both of which aroused considerable agitation. One of them would certainly have led to a strike had it not been for the intervention of trade union officials.

The first was the case of Marshall, a shop steward at Parkhead. There had been some trouble and a short strike in one section over non-unionists, and Marshall was accused of " slacking and causing others to slack." Early in July he was sentenced to three months' imprisonment.

A few nights later I attended a meeting of our leading committee at the Herald League Bookshop. Owing to a meeting at the factory, I was late in arriving. I sat down beside Tommy Clark, who had been acting as chairman in my absence. The meeting was being addressed by someone I had never seen before. As he spoke I looked at him with amazement. At the end of every other sentence he would compress his lips tightly, and look around to see how the others were taking it. He was reporting on the Marshall case.

" I went up to Mr. Chisholm," he informed us (I had missed the first part), " and I said to Mr. Chisholm, ' You've got to do something, or there's nae saying what'll happen here.' ' I can't do anything,' says Mr. Chisholm. 'Then I'll see Sir William,' I said. Up ah goes tae see Sir William." I whispered to Tommy Clark, "Who the hell is this?" "It's Davy Kirkwood from Parkhead," Tommy replied.

That was my first meeting with Kirkwood, as it was his first entry into the life of the leaders' group of the Clyde Workers' Committee. He was a big, generous, clean-living fellow, for whom I had, and have, considerable regard; but his pronounced egotism, played upon by other influences, became our undoing later. But despite all the talk with Mr. Chisholm and Sir William, nothing happened, and it was only when he brought the matter before the committee that steps were taken that secured the release of Marshall.

The other case, that of the Fairfield shipwrights, was one of greater moment to the workers of the Clyde. This was a case where a group of shipwrights acting under the union instructions refused to do a certain job, were hauled before a munitions court and sentenced to thirty days' imprisonment or a £10 fine. Three of them, McPherson, Fleming and Turner, refused to pay the fine and went to prison. The union officials immediately took up the fight on their behalf and we decided to support them in the call for strike action, which all of us expected them to start. Instead, they made statements to the Press, sent deputations here and there and had interviews with all kinds of important individuals.

Fairfield's was ready to take action and if Fairfield's had been called out, the others would immediately have joined.

So strong indeed was the demand for action that the officials called a conference of District Committees in the Christian Institute. As an official of my union I attended. The conference had been called and was controlled by a group of permanent officials, including Sharp of the Boilermakers, Brodie and Buntin of the A.S.E., Lorrimer of the Blacksmiths, and a number of others who occupied the platform.

Sharp, in the chair, opened the meeting and warned us about the serious situation that confronted us and about the fact that there was a war going on.

" Yes, the class war," the boys shouted.

Sharp tried to evade that and went on about our responsibilities and how we should not be led away by irresponsible revolutionaries. It was obvious some wangle was being prepared. All present could feel that. Sharp could not continue for the noise, so he called in Lorrimer to read a resolution. Lorrimer did so and it left us gasping. There was a protest about the imprisonment in it, but it was addressed to Mr. Asquith (the Prime Minister) and appealed to him to secure the liberation of the shipwrights.

We could scarcely believe we had heard aright. I immediately scribbled out a short resolution calling on Fairfield's to stop work and the other undertakings to support Fairfield's and proposed it as alternative resolution.

" No alternative resolutions will be accepted," said Mr. Sharp.

" All right," I said, " I'll propose it as an addendum to your resolution."

" No addendum accepted," Sharp replied.

" Can I move an amendment? " a delegate asked.

" No amendments will be accepted," was the answer.

Then pandemonium broke loose. The trick was plain. They had been leading us " up the garden " under the belief that they intended to call a strike and had used the opportunity given them to demoralize our forces. For over an hour there was a scene of wild confusion. Sharp tried to get order and to get his resolution considered, but nobody would have it.

" Let us try to conduct our meeting a little more harmoniously," he shouted during a lull.

" Mr. Chairman," I called, " I'll make a proposal that should restore harmony." Everybody quieted down. " I propose the platform party for a song," I said. Not very bright, I'll admit, but it served to express the disgust that I and others felt. There was a roar of laughter and cheering and the platform party gave up, the meeting ending with Lorrimer holding on to his precious resolution.

Lorrimer came over to me and said, " You've a bloody hard cheek." " What's the matter now? " I asked him. " You propose the platform party

for a song," he repeated, " you think that's funny."
What I said to Lorrimer had better remain un-
printed.

But they had succeeded in their design. Before
we could get our forces ready for independent
action, the shipwrights had served their term and
were out amongst us once again.

CHAPTER V

THE activity in the factories was but a part of the general activity going on everywhere around Glasgow. McLean had become a figure known to everyone. His classes were packed with eager students, his meetings were the scenes of wild revolutionary enthusiasm. I was still one of his closest associates despite the trouble over Petrov, and spoke with him at all the principal demonstrations. In spite of the frenzied attempts of the patriots and the Press, it was impossible to whip up opposition to McLean. Any patriots who were about considered it wise to keep away from McLean's meetings.

And there were patriots in Glasgow all right. But somehow they never could get going. Meetings were attempted, but these generally ended up in demonstrations against the war. Then as demobilized soldiers began to stream back to the area, the patriots felt that at last they had got a weapon they could use against the workers. The Discharged and Demobilized Soldiers' and Sailors' Federation was formed to protect and care for those who had done their bit and were now released from service.

In the beginning a " patriot " got himself elected as secretary and endeavoured to keep the movement away from working-class influence, but many of those who were most active in the Federation had been active in the workshops up till the outbreak of war, and now they took up the struggle anew. We soon had a majority of " rebels " in the Executive and later on got the " patriotic " secretary removed and one of our fellows elected in his place. There was no help for the war-makers from the Discharged Soldiers' Federation in Glasgow. It was soon supporting all the resolutions of the Clyde Workers' Committee and of other anti-war bodies as well as passing strongly-worded resolutions on its own.

An attempt was made to build a " patriotic " anti-working-class organization, the leader of which was a rather futile individual named Jamieson. He used to hold meetings on a Sunday night at the foot of Buchanan Street, but the crowd who attended went there to watch the antics of a very precocious little fellow named Wratten. This little chap was about fourteen years of age, but already he had imbibed quite an amount of pacifist and anti-war phrases and he let them go every Sunday night at Jamieson's meeting. Occasionally he turned up with a packet full of crackers, the kind that go off with a bang when they are thrown on the ground. He would stand in the centre of the ring and when Jamieson came out with anything particularly forceful, he would shout " Ha, ha," and bang would go a cracker. Although worried by the youngster, Jamieson managed to carry on for quite a while until he tried to develop an offensive—of which more later—which ended in his complete ruin.

Following the promulgation of the Defence of the Realm Act and the many arrests that resulted, an organization had been formed for the protection of civil liberties. It was to a large extent composed of intellectuals and petty-bourgeois pacifists. As there was no strength behind it, the members had to look to the shop stewards for backing in anything they might attempt.

Through this organization a meeting was once called in the Charing Cross Hall, towards the end of Sauchiehall Street. The principal speaker was J. R. MacDonald, who was then being everywhere attacked in the Press, quite wrongly, as a " defeatist and traitor." MacDonald's position, like Snowden's, was peculiar. While the Labour Party had decided for support of the Government in the prosecution of the war, it was impossible for either of these openly to accept this decision. Both depended for their political existence on maintaining their leadership of the I.L.P., and as the bulk of the active leaders of the I.L.P. in the districts were young school teachers or petty-bourgeois pacifists, they had to choose a very careful path in connection with the war. MacDonald's notorious volubility stood him in good stead during this period. He could talk and talk without end, creating the impression that he was saying things of the greatest moment, whilst actually only spreading confusion among his hearers. Nevertheless, the Press had made him appear as a great figure against the war, so Glasgow was prepared to give him a welcome.

As the shop stewards had to be brought in to protect the meeting, I was invited to speak. So also was Shinwell, who was then chairman of the Glasgow Trades Council.

At this meeting Jamieson saw his chance; he would attack the lion in its lair. With his supporters around him, he held an open-air meeting at Wellington Street, just a short distance from the Charing Cross Hall, and by a frenzied attack on MacDonald soon gathered a considerable crowd. He then informed his audience that he and his supporters were going to march to the meeting and force their way in. The crowd thought this was a great idea and gave Jamieson quite a cheer. Off he set, with a huge crowd following, right to the entrance to the hall. From the door of the hall in Sauchiehall Street to the hall proper there is a long corridor. This corridor was occupied by stewards by the time Jamieson arrived, while the hall inside was already crowded. MacDonald was in the platform ante-room and when the shouts from outside penetrated he became very nervous. He had already had experience of a not very happy character of similar demonstrations in England. He asked us if there was a rear way out. I told him there was nothing to worry about; that the crowd outside was quite good-natured and would give him a cheer if he went out.

But he was very doubtful about it. Then McGovern came in and took off his coat. From his inside pocket he extracted a short, heavy piece of lead pipe. MacDonald looked at the weapon and smiled. Maxton remarked, " He's a pacifist."

" That's the sort of pacifist I like to see," said MacDonald.

The roars became louder outside and MacDonald's nervousness increased. I gave a nod to Shinwell and we went out along the corridor to the front door. I opened one half of the door and there was Jamieson right up against it with his immediate lieutenants gathered around him. Right over to the other side of the street a great crowd was surging, and thoroughly enjoying itself.

Jamieson shouted, to the delight of the laughing crowd: " As a citizen I demand admittance to this meeting."

" Oh, you want in," I said.

" Yes, I want in," he retorted.

" All right," I said, " come in."

But he had got a look inside and the sight had not been encouraging. Instead of pressing forward he drew back and then the situation got really funny. Shinwell and several others made a grab and got hold of Jamieson and one of his colleagues and started pulling them in. Jamieson let out a yell of " Help! " and put up a heroic struggle not to get in. This was too much for the crowd. They roared with laughter. Jamieson and his supporters were only too glad to get away.

Inside the hall MacDonald got a great reception, talked a lot in his best and most confusing manner and the meeting passed off without any untoward incident. But, immediately after the meeting, Jamieson and a colleague applied for and obtained summonses for assault, one against Shinwell, the other against a comrade named Morris Nyman. Very cunningly, they had chosen two Jewish comrades with a view to arousing prejudice. But, while Morris Nyman, who came up before an ordinary bailie on a charge of assault was fined twenty shillings, Shinwell, on a charge of assaulting Jamieson, came up before a stipendiary magistrate who, when he heard the evidence, told the prosecuting fiscal he had the wrong man in the dock and dismissed the case.

But Jamieson had another try. A few Sundays later he held a meeting at the same spot, Wellington Street, and after " piling on the agony," he declared his intention of going along to Charing Cross, where an open-air peace meeting was being held, to " finish the pacifists." He got to Charing Cross all right, with the intention of making trouble, and he made trouble—for himself. From Charing Cross he went to hospital and after a period of meditation there, he decided to seek other fields for his activities. Glasgow knew him and the Scottish Patriotic League no more.

Another attempt to get some sort of " patriotic " organization going in Scotland was an effort by Sir Charles B. Renshaw, at one time a very pro-

minent figure in the West of Scotland. This took
the form of the Scottish Food Economy League.
While the decision to set it going had been taken
by Sir Charles and a number of " big-wigs " in
Edinburgh, the actual first effort to approach
Glasgow was made in my home town, Paisley. A
meeting was called by invitation, at the Council
Chambers. To this meeting the Trades Council
was invited to send two representatives. This to
give it the necessary democratic touch. I and
another comrade, John Mercer, were appointed as
the Trades Council representatives, with instructions
to do whatever we thought necessary to prevent any
anti-working-class organization being formed.

Jock Mercer and I duly attended and found
ourselves in strange company. A local parson
occupied the chair. He opened the proceedings
with a few general remarks about the distinguished
and representative character of the meeting; then
he called on Sir Charles to say his piece. Sir Charles
did so. He talked about the cost of the war, of the
sacrifice we were all called upon to make and how
we could save enormous sums through economy in
cooking food and saving food and so on. When he
finished, the chairman, with all due deference,
invited Sir Thomas Glen Coats to speak. It is not
seemly to speak ill of the dead, but it may be permitted to say that Sir Thomas wasn't too well
supplied with " intellect." He stuttered and splut-
tered but succeeded in making it clear that the
workers had got to be stopped from wasting food.

They were getting too much money and were simply throwing it away. He was followed by Provost Robertson, of " Marmalade " fame. He was a typical little sycophant, ready to grovel at the feet of the " great " family, the cotton-thread Coats. He dotted the " i's " and crossed the " t's " of Sir Thomas and then he gave us this gem. " A young minister in the town was going around collecting money for a new Church Hall. He knocked at the door of a worker's house in an ordinary tenement. A woman opened the door and he explained what he was after. ' Well,' she said, ' you look a nice young man and it's for a good object, so ah'll gie ye something.' She walked over, took something off the mantelpiece and handed it to him. He looked at it with astonishment. It was a roll of notes. He counted them. Thirty. Thirty one-pound notes. ' My good woman,' he gasped, ' this is too much.' ' Tak' it,' she said, ' tak' it, that's only one week's pay.' "

Mercer and I listened to trash like this for quite a time. After the Provost came a fashionable physician, then a lawyer, then a lady or two and the sum total of it all was the need for setting up an influential committee to advise workers on how to economize in food.

When the chairman had got off his list of names, he informed us that we had heard all sides and that it now remained for us to appoint the committee.

" Excuse me, Mr. Chairman," I interjected, " so far you've only heard one side. I now propose to

let you hear the other side." " Hear, hear," Jock
Mercer chipped in with very strong emphasis.
The chairman looked round in a helpless sort of
way and then slowly subsided into his seat. I then
sailed into them one after another. Sir Thomas
couldn't stand it. He jumped up in a rage and
bounced out of the Chamber. As for the Provost,
I attacked him roundly. I ended by declaring that
if any committee was appointed the Trades Council
would see that it was a committee of workers and
that its job would be to go round the Coats' gang and
the Robertsons, deprive them of their servants, all of
whom could be found useful employment elsewhere
and thus give their " ladies " the opportunity of
practising economy in the kitchen and the washtub.

When I finished there was general agreement that
committees didn't do any good. The chairman
looked round, not knowing what to do, but couldn't
catch anybody's eye or get any help from any of
those present, so he abruptly declared the meeting
closed. That was the end of that effort. It was never
heard of again, except that on the following day
the local paper gave a report of the meeting. It
gave quite a lot of space to Sir Charles, a fair amount
to Sir Thomas, a little less to the Provost and then
finished by saying: " Mr. Gallacher also spoke."
Thus the Press " truthfully " reports.

These are only some incidents of the year 1915
—a year full of activity inside and outside the
factories; activity that was causing the greatest

concern to the Government and the military authorities. It was towards the end of this year that word came that the Minister of Munitions, D. Lloyd George, was going to pay us a visit and we set about making our preparations to give him a fitting reception.

CHAPTER VI

THE CLYDE IN WARTIME

THE war was taking heavy toll of the young manhood of Europe. Gone was the " romance " —the glory of war. Instead, shattered flesh, clotted blood, slime and filth. Men driven to their death, driven into a revolting slaughter-house. Military strategy there was none. The generals, dull and bovine, knew but one refrain: " More men, more men." The fields of death were hungry, thousands each day must die. But how to get the men? Every trick was tried. Young men first—the older ones used to drive them in. Categories, " non-essential " and " essential," used against them. When every method to drive the young men to their death " voluntarily " had been exhausted, the need was greater than ever. Conscription was more and more openly advocated.

I remember speaking at a meeting on Glasgow Green and drawing attention to a speech of Churchill. He had been talking about me, I said, and I didn't like what he had to say. His words had been, " We will sacrifice our last shilling and our *last man*." One of the workers present interjected, " You're wrong, Willie, he wasn't talking about you, he was talking about himself."

77

But the drain of men from industry had been very great. It was going to be greater. The question of supplying the factories with labour had become an urgent one. Where could workers be found?

The answer soon came—women. " Dilution of labour " was the official title of the process. Lloyd George, Minister of Munitions, addressed a meeting of employers in Manchester at the beginning of December 1915, and dealt with this question. Then, in answer to one of the employers who had drawn attention to the unions, he said, " You go ahead, and if the trade unions interfere, I'll deal with them." I took careful note of that statement, and filed it away for further reference.

Towards the middle of December we were informed quite definitely that he would visit Glasgow for two or three days at Christmas, in order to get into personal touch with the factories, ending with a conference on " dilution " on Christmas Day. The exact arrangements for his visit were not made known till the last moment, but on Wednesday, December 22, two or three of the permanent trade union officials from Glasgow travelled to Newcastle, at the invitation of the Minister, to discuss the project he had in view. These officials had lost all sense of responsibility to the working class. They asked but one thing of Lloyd George, that he should not have anything to do with the nightmare of their lives, the Clyde Workers' Committee. This he readily promised, and a statement was published in the Press that the Minister of Munitions during his visit to Clyde would not recognize, directly or indirectly, the " unofficial " body known as the Clyde Workers' Committee. He was a great little fellow—in Newcastle!

We called a special delegate meeting for Thursday night, the 23rd. For this meeting I drew up a short resolution, which we hurriedly ran off as a leaflet. The resolution declared the loyal support of the shop stewards for the policy of the Clyde Workers' Committee, and the decision to attend the so-called conference, called by the Minister of Munitions, but only to participate in it on the lines laid down by the Committee.

That same Thursday Lloyd George arrived in Glasgow. His first visit was to Parkhead. Sir William Beardmore sent for Kirkwood and asked him to call the shop stewards together to meet the Minister. This Kirkwood did, but it was a mistake; a mistake that was repeated at a later stage with disastrous results. When they were gathered together, Kirkwood introduced Lloyd George as an enemy of the workers, and as a lawyer, ending up with the statement that one engineer was worth a dozen lawyers. Quite unabashed, Lloyd George did his stuff, although he had quite a lot of difficulty in getting it over. At the conclusion of his talk a fellow set up a camera.

Tommy Clark asked in an ominous voice: " What's this? "

" We've to get a photograph taken," said Lloyd George.

" There'll be no bloody photograph here! " declared Tommy ; then, to the photographer, " Get to hell out of it! "

The photographer got. In his memoirs, Lloyd George describes Tommy as a " natural savage." If only he was to see him now!

From Parkhead he went to Weir's. He wasn't feeling too good, but he looked to his friend Weir to help him out. The convenor of shop stewards, Comrade Smith, was sent for. Lloyd George wanted to meet and talk with the shop stewards, he was told. To this he replied: " We have had a meeting of the shop stewards and they don't want to meet or talk with Lloyd George."

" What ? " they exclaimed. " You can't do this. Think of what it means. Please go and see them again. It's terrible, terrible. Get them to change their decision and meet him, if only for a minute."

Smith went away and returned some time later. " Aren't they coming ? " he was asked. " No," he replied, " they aren't coming. If Mr. Lloyd George wants to discuss conditions on the Clyde, he'll have to discuss them with the Clyde Workers' Committee."

It was a complete knock-out for the Minister of Munitions. His tour of conquest had come to a sorry end. The following day he crept into one or two places where our organization was not so strong, but to such places as the Albion he gave a wide berth.

At our meeting at night, held in the Central Halls, Bath Street, there was a full turn out, but I had to leave before it got started. I had a heavy night's work before me. While I was chairman of the Clyde Workers' Committee, I was still an executive member of my union, and therefore had the right to attend the official meetings. And there was an official meeting that same night. It was held in the A.S.E. Hall at Carlton Place. When I got along, they were all gathered there—sixty or seventy of them.

Sharp, Lorrimer and Buntin were at the table at the end of the hall, sorting out bundles of tickets. When they had the tickets sorted out to their liking, Sharp reported on the visit to Newcastle. He told us that the Minister had asked them to arrange a meeting of the shop stewards for Saturday, the 25th, in St. Andrew's Hall, the tickets for which he had supplied, and these were now before us, so many for each union. The Minister had agreed to pay each shop steward 7s. 6d. for expenses, so that they would have to be careful in distributing tickets, as each one represented that amount.

As soon as he had finished, Harry Hill, of the Shipwrights, walked up to the table, got his tickets, and turned to leave the hall. I jumped to my feet and said, " Brother Chairman, before Brother Hill leaves with those tickets, we've got to discuss and decide whether we're going to have anything to do with the meeting." There was quite a commotion following this, in the midst of which Hill went stamping out of the hall. But he was scarcely out when the door burst open and he was back in.

" There's your tickets," he shouted. " To hell wi' them, and to hell wi' you. By Christ, I never met your equal for making trouble! " He slammed the tickets down and went banging out again. We all had a laugh at this, after which I addressed the meeting.

I quoted from the speech at Manchester already referred to, and then asked: " Have we no sense of responsibility to the organizations we represent? Are we to be at the beck and call of this avowed enemy of the trade union movement? To what are we being reduced when this man can send along tickets and instruct us to organize a meeting for him? "

I followed this up with a series of arguments against their participation in the meeting. One after the other, they followed, endorsing my remarks and opposing any support for Lloyd George or participation in the meeting.

The discussion went on till ten o'clock, when a vote was taken; about sixty voted against participation and five for. When Buntin saw how the vote was going, he went dashing into the corridor, got hold of the 'phone and rang up the Central Station Hotel, where Lloyd George, with his tame trade union and Labour Party officials, had his headquarters.

He came back into the hall as the meeting was breaking up and asked for a hearing on a matter of great urgency. He then informed us that he had been on the 'phone to the hotel and that Mr. Arthur Henderson had begged him to have the meeting give him the opportunity of a few words. I wasn't averse to Henderson coming over. In fact I wanted a few words with him; so, more by way of a joke than anything, I said, " Tell him we'll wait if he'll provide us with taxis after the meeting's over." There was general laughter and cheering at this suggestion. Sam Buntin took it very solemnly, and after another short interlude at the 'phone, informed us that " Mr. Henderson thanks you very much, and he has instructed his secretary to order a fleet of taxis." Yes, sir, they had money to burn.

In a few minutes, Henderson and a couple of others arrived. After a few words from the chairman he made a pathetic appeal to us to assist Lloyd George in the great fight he was making to win the war.

When he had finished, I produced my clipping of the Manchester speech, and asked him if it meant that the Cabinet was going to attack the trade unions. No, he replied, it was a personal expression on the part of Lloyd George. I then asked if there were no such thing as Cabinet responsibility, and, if Lloyd George could publicly voice this personal expression, would Henderson publicly repudiate it, also as a " personal expression "? He hedged on this, but other officials joined in and demanded that he, as a trade unionist, publicly repudiate Lloyd George's anti-trade-union statement. He refused to do so.

I then said, " Isn't it clear that Henderson isn't here as a free agent? He is permitted to come and speak to us as the servant of one of our worst enemies. How is it possible that a man can fall so low? Fellow members, let us send him back with a message to his master that the Clyde trade unionists are not the lackeys of the workers' enemies." There were shouts of " Hear, hear! " and " Vote! " The vote was then taken, with the same result as previously.

Henderson had fallen down on his job. He was wild, blazing mad; but not as mad as I was some ten years later, when, at the Liverpool Labour Party Conference, Aitken Ferguson and I were discussing some questions with the Standing Orders Committee; Henderson, apropos of something I had said, remarked with the lofty air of one whose soul was unsullied by the follies and misdeeds of lesser men, " Those of us who have guarded the movement in the past, can be trusted to guard its welfare in the future."

I looked at Fergie, I looked at the other, then I burst out with: " By God, you're brazen. You've got the damned impudence to say that to me. Why you snivelling humbug, I was guarding and fighting for the Labour Movement when you were standing on the ' doormat.' " He turned chalky white, and while the other members of the Standing Orders

Committee were still gasping, he got up and left the room.

That, however, was in 1925. When we finished with him that night in 1915, we went out, and there in Carlton Place the taxis were all drawn up. I had seven miles to go to Paisley; Prentice of the Brassmoulder's travelled in the same direction, to the "half-way" between Paisley and Glasgow. We travelled together and had some good laughs on the way. Prentice tried to open the door, and smashed the glass in the process. "What's that?" shouted the driver. "Just another bob or two on Henderson's account," said Prentice.

When I got home, about midnight, I found a report of the Central Hall meeting waiting for me. Everything had gone according to plan.

The following morning, Friday, the 24th, I was up at my usual time, 4.30 a.m. That was the hour at which most of us had to start the day in order to get across the Clyde for six o'clock.

When I got to the factory, I had to report to the shop stewards the events of the previous day. Johnny Muir and I had taken the day off on the Thursday, and made a tour of the shops ahead of Lloyd George. All morning there was a buzz of excitement throughout the departments. The question was being continually put by one or another, "Do you think he'll come to the Albion?" I replied that I didn't think so, but that we were ready for him if he should. If he had come, not only would he have found that the shop stewards refused to meet him, but that we were all set to stop the factory as a demonstration against him.

About 8.45 the manager sent for me. I went up to the office, and he said, " There's a 'phone message from the Central Station Hotel. Lord Murray wants you."

" Oh, does he? " I said.

" Look here, Gallacher," said the manager, " what's going on at all? What does he want you for? "

" That's too long a story for now," I replied. " You'll hear all about it later."

I reported the matter to the shop stewards and then got a tramcar up to the city. When I got to the hotel I found a group of officials at the entrance. I had scarcely joined them when who should come barging along but Harry Hill, with a pleasant smile on his broad cheery face. He shook hands and said, " How are you, Willie? " just as though we had parted the best of friends the night before.

" But what are we here for this morning? " he continued.

" I suppose they think they're going to talk us into changing our minds," I said.

" What do they think we are? " shouted Harry. " Do they think we've nothing else to do but run after them! Tell them our decision stands, and finish with them."

By this time most of the officials had arrived, so we went up to our meeting. Lloyd George was absent, so Lord Murray took charge of the pro-

ceedings. Tables were set to form a square. Lord
Murray, Henderson and some more of Lloyd
George's outfit sat along the top. Buntin, Sharpe,
Lorrimer and Whitehead sat along the side to the
right of the chairman, while the rest of us sat around
the bottom and the left or on chairs at the rear of
the room.

Lord Murray opened the proceedings with the
customary recital—about the need for men and for
munitions. He told us what a wonderful man
Lloyd George was and how much he sympathized
with the workers; how under normal circumstances
he would do anything for the workers, but now his
one thought was victory in the war. Would we
help him?

When he finished, he and the others looked at
me, so I took the floor. I started off with, " None
of us here is prepared to accept the statement that
Lloyd George is, or ever was, a friend of the
workers. If he's so keen on winning the war, let
him tackle the employers, stop their profits. They're
piling up profits at our expense. However, that's
our war, the war against the employers. We don't
mind him being with them. It's what we expect,
but when he asks us to assist him in carrying through
their plans, that's treating us cheap, to say the least
of it. We stand for the workers we represent, and
while there are employers reaping profits we'll carry
on the war against them."

Bailie Whitehead jumped to his feet and, in his
best City Council manner, addressed the Chair:

" My Lord Murray," said the Bailie, " this man is out for bloody revolution. He is not here representing trade unionists. He is here representing a group of irresponsible revolutionaries like himself, and they don't care whether the war is won or not."

Two or three of the others started shouting across at Whitehead, and it took some time before the chairman could get order restored. Then Sam Buntin slowly raised himself from his seat. He had something to say and he meant to say it.

" My lord." A pause; then, pointing a finger at me, " This man has been repudiated by his own colleagues." Sam meant to create a sensation and he succeeded.

" What do you mean? " queried Lord Murray.

" My lord," said Sam, " while he was at our meeting last night getting us to turn down the Lloyd George meeting, his own committee met in the Central Hall and decided to carry on with it. A group of them came round to our hall this morning and took away the tickets."

Lord Murray looked at him in consternation. He immediately realized what the slower-witted Sam had failed to grasp—Lloyd George was in the hands of the Philistines.

" Is this true? " he asked me. " Have you tickets? "

" We have," I replied.

" Excuse me, gentlemen," he said; and went into the adjoining room to consult Lloyd George, who had just returned to the hotel. In a few minutes he came back, Lloyd George with him. He gazed coldly at the company and said, " That'll be all, gentlemen, good day." And then, " Mr. Gallacher, will you please wait for a moment? "

So they were dismissed without a word of apology or explanation. They were " fine fellows " when they could be of use, but they could now no longer be of service.

All those who had voted against participation were delighted at the turn of events. They were glad to escape any association with the meeting and they knew what our distribution of tickets meant for Lloyd George. But Sharp, Buntin and the other " patriots " went away feeling miserable. Later on, however, Sharp got a job as technical advisor to the employers, and Buntin got into the Glasgow office of the Labour Ministry.

When they had all gone Lord Murray and Lloyd George came over to me.

" Can you get in touch with the members of your committee? " Lloyd George asked.

" Yes," I replied.

" Will you arrange for me to meet them this evening? "

" I will," I answered. " We'll meet you here at seven o'clock."

" Thank you, Mr. Gallacher! Thank you! " He was very effusive.

The word was sent round and the committee

met at 6.30. We had a short session putting the final touches to our arrangements. Then at seven o'clock we entered the room where the session had been held during the day. Lloyd George occupied the central position at the top table, with his colleagues on either side. I was his opposite number at the bottom table, with Johnny Muir, Kirkwood and McManus on my right; Messer, Tommy Clark and some others on my left. We had also added to the committee two women workers.

The first act of the Minister was to pass around a box of cigars. His own crowd dutifully took theirs but we refused them. Some of us took out our pipes. Lloyd George, always ready to take a trick, stuck his hand in his pocket, brought out a pipe, and said, " That's right, boys. Why should we be formal? If we are going to talk, let us be comfortable; and what's more comforting than a good pipe? "

" What's the procedure you propose? " I asked.

" Well," he replied, beaming on us, " I thought it would be best if I made a statement giving my views on the situation. Then you could ask what questions you felt were urgent, following which we could agree about the procedure for the meeting to-morrow."

" We cannot accept that," I said. " We propose that you make your statement. Then we shall present our views. We shall then see if it is possible to come to an agreement on the all-important question of control of dilution. That's our proposition." After a short time, this was agreed. It was either that or finish, before we started.

This much agreed upon, Lloyd George got going. He gave us a typical propaganda speech. About the ravages of the war, of the deadly nature of machine-gunning from pill-boxes, of our determination to carry on till victory, but that munitions were the key to victory. We were short of men to man the factories at present operating; new factories had to be built. Therefore thousands of new workers were needed, and we had to find them. He looked to us for support. As he looked at us he could see that strong spirit of independence that would never tolerate the military domination of Germany. Yes, he knew that we were the very men to rely upon in a crisis.

Such, in general, was the line he took. Yet only a couple of days earlier he had stated to the Press that under no circumstances would he have anything to do with us.

I said a few words to the effect that all he had told us was already well known; and then called on Johnny Muir to state our case.

Johnny was masterly in the handling of the subject. He dealt very briefly with the development of capitalism and with the fact that the one and only concern of the employers was profit; that in pursuit of profit every change in the method of production was used to cheapen the cost, and that this took the form of continually introducing new types of semi-skilled or unskilled labour at the lowest possible rate of wages. Thus he showed that dilution had always been a feature of capitalist development.

Now, however, he continued, the speeding of production necessitated by the war had made an extraordinary acceleration of this process an urgent necessity. All this we understood. We weren't trying to stop the process. On the contrary, we were all in favour of encouraging it. But we had to take note of the fact that large-scale dilution would be used by the employers to introduce cheap labour and by this means force a general all-round lowering of standards. Against anything like this we would fight with all our power. The position therefore stood as follows: the Minister wanted a large influx of new labour, dilution. We had no objection to this. The only question at issue between us was: who was going to control the process—the employers or the workers? The Minister had said that he held no brief for the employers. His one concern was to win the war. We therefore proposed that the Government take over the factories, right out of the hands of the employers, and put the full control of all matters relating to wages, working conditions and the introduction of new labour, into the hands of the factory committees.

Such, in short, was the case Johnny so ably presented. While he was speaking, the pompous little peacock at the top of the room was doing everything to distract attention. I have never in all my life seen such a pitiful example of uncontrollable conceit. He brushed at his moustache, he pawed at his hair, looking around to see if he was the centre of attention. His " yes-men " played up to him. They had their eyes on him, not on Johnny Muir. Then, to crown it all, he turned to Henderson, on his right, and started whispering. This meant that he was half-turned away from Johnny Muir.

I suddenly said, " That'll do, Johnny. Stop! "

Johnny stopped. They all sat up with a start. Addressing Lloyd George, I remarked, " Excuse me, Mr. Lloyd George. If you don't want to hear us, we'll go. We're not here to waste our time."

" But I've been listening," he hurriedly exclaimed. " I've heard every word."

" You haven't been listening," I said. " All the boys here know you haven't. As for you, Henderson, you ought to be ashamed of yourself. You, a trade unionist, lending yourself to such indifference when a fellow trade unionist is stating a difficult case. Either you give Johnny attention or we go."

" Please go on, Mr. Muir," Lloyd George begged. " It's very interesting."

" Go ahead, Johnny! " I said.

So Johnny went on to his conclusion with the whole top table's attention directed towards him.

When he had finished, I called on Kirkwood to say a few words. Kirkwood said: " I think I gave him enough yesterday out at Parkhead, so I'll content myself with saying that I stand by every word uttered by Johnny Muir. He's presented the right question: Who's going to control the factories?

And I tell you, Mr. Lloyd George, Minister of Munitions, we are."

I then asked McManus to speak. He made it short and very effective. Johnny Muir had stated the committee's case. There could be no misunderstanding of where we stood on that question. But in view of the speech made by Lloyd George which was mostly pro-war propaganda, it would be as well to let him know where we stood on this. We knew it was a war for trade and territory, said McManus, a war carried on for the purposes of imperialism. We were not supporting any such war. We opposed it. Therefore, there was no possibility of getting us to yield in the slightest degree, on any issue affecting conditions in the industry, by any appeal based on the need for winning the war. If that were understood, we should be in a better position to face the only question before us: Who is going to control dilution?

After the two women had each said a few words, Lloyd George took the floor. He was really expansive in his praise of Johnny Muir. Rarely had it been his pleasure to hear a case so clearly and ably put, but the proposals were impossible; he couldn't consider them.

" Why not? " I interjected.

" Because," he replied, " it would mean a revolution, and you can't carry through a revolution in the midst of a war."

It was only a couple of years later, however, that

Lenin and the Bolsheviks showed him just how that very thing could be done.

We were able to show Lloyd George that he was proving our argument. If the employers had to choose between losing the war and losing their profits, they'd stop the war and fight for their profits. He didn't like it—not one little bit—and he soon brought the discussion to a close. The next item was the meeting on the following day.

He then proposed the following, without a smile. Henderson as chairman would speak for twenty minutes; then Lloyd George would speak for about sixty minutes, after which he would answer a few written questions. And this was termed on the tickets a " conference " on dilution!

We told him he could never get away with anything like that. The shop stewards wouldn't stand for a propaganda speech on the war. They were coming to discuss the conditions under which dilution would be introduced and they would see to it that that, and nothing else, was the subject considered. We proposed two minutes for Henderson to introduce the speakers. Then half an hour for Lloyd George to state his views on the new labour forces, and Johnny Muir to follow with a statement on our views; after which discussion would take place on the floor.

This was a clear, straightforward proposal, if it were to be a conference such as he himself had called for. Did he consider it? Not a bit!

" All right," we said. " Nobody can stop you

from having your own way. You can decide what you and Henderson propose doing, but you can't make the shop stewards listen to you."

"Oh," he said, quite cocky. "They'll listen to me."

"You're in for the surprise of your life," we told him.

But nothing could change his mind, so the meeting broke up.

We were to have yet further evidence of his colossal egotism before we finally finished with him. He had become so accustomed to "yes-men" and lackeys that he had come to believe that a few soft words, with a hint of favours to come, was sufficient for anyone. We were out of the hall, and were donning our hats and coats, when one of the secretaries came running out.

"Oh, Mr. Gallacher," as he got his eye on me, "Mr. Lloyd George would like to have a word with you."

I asked the boys whether I should go. Yes, they said, see what he's got to say. So I went back in.

All the troop had gone, leaving only Lord Murray with Lloyd George. When I walked over, the latter put his arm round my shoulder in a familiar manner. He told me I was a great fellow. That it was obvious I had won the confidence of my colleagues. He was sure there was a great future ahead of me. I let him go on for a bit and then asked what he wanted. He was very anxious

that the meeting the following day should be a
success. It would be a tragedy if anything went
wrong. He wanted to make a personal appeal to
me for my support. He would see that I didn't
regret it. Would I come on the platform with
him?

I replied that I would go on the platform if he
accepted our conditions: half an hour for himself,
then Johnny Muir, followed by an open discussion.

He got irritated at this. " Conditions, conditions,
conditions! You know I can't accept such conditions."

" Well," I said, " you can't get our support, and,
believe me, you won't get anywhere without it."

" I can't talk to you—you're impossible," he
barked, and went barging out of the room. Lord
Murray looked the picture of misery.

" Now," I said, " is that the way to behave?
He asks me in, and then treats me like that."
Murray shook his head and said, " I'm sorry you
could not come to an agreement." We shook hands
and I left him standing there, brooding. I got
back among the boys and reported what had happened. Did we laugh?

.   .   .   .   .

Saturday, December 25, Christmas Day, and
all eyes turned towards St. Andrew's Hall, where
the modern St. George was going to slay the dragon
of unrest and conquer the unruly Clyde.

The hall soon filled with shop stewards and when

they entered what a sight met their gaze! The balcony of the hall continues right on to the tier of seats above the platform, so that, under ordinary circumstances, anyone in the balcony can move down on to the platform. But—not on Christmas Day, 1915! On each side of the balcony, a few feet above the platform tier, which was unoccupied during the proceedings, powerful barricades had been erected; while, lined right across the hall in front of the platform, were several rows of policemen. St. George had himself well protected.

Our boys now started singing. They kept it going till the platform party came on, and then all got to their feet and the " Red Flag " was sung, the platform having to stand to the finish.

Henderson then stepped forward to speak, and the storm broke. Roar after roar at the hapless Henderson. After vain attempts to be heard, he made a gesture, and Lloyd George got up. He pranced up and down the platform; he waved his arms; he stretched them out in mute appeal.

In a moment of comparative quiet, he shouted, " I appeal to you in the name of my old friend, the late Keir Hardie! "

At the mention of Keir Hardie's name, the " Red Flag " was sung again. He stormed and threatened, he screamed and shouted till the sweat ran down his face, but it was all of no use. When he stopped through sheer exhaustion, the signal was given and Johnny Muir got up on a seat.

There was instantaneous silence as Johnny started

to speak on the actual questions for which we had been called together. Henderson, Lloyd George and the others walked off the platform, leaving the meeting in our hands. Immediately after the meeting, the Ministry of Munitions issued an " official " report to the Press. The Glasgow *Forward* published a true report and was immediately suppressed.

Comment has often been made by British journalists regarding the slavish conditions of the Nazi Press, as if it were something entirely foreign to the British conception of journalism. But the British Press can be just as venal and submissive as the German. That is one of the lessons learned from the last European war.

But while Tom Johnston, who owned the *Forward*, published that story and paid for doing so with several weeks' suppression, he looked with great disfavour upon the Clyde Workers' Committee, except of course, when it was providing protection for pacifist meetings. It had been obvious for some time that we had to get a paper of our own. The Lloyd George meeting provided the opportunity. We got quite a number of those who attended to apply for the seven and sixpence expenses money, and then to hand it over to a fund for our paper.

By the middle of January 1916 our paper, *The Worker*, appeared, with Johnny Muir as editor. Our printers were the Socialist Labour Party Press, in Renfrew Street. Surely there was never a paper so well received! Bundles going into the factories were eagerly bought by the workers. Those of us who were writing for it put our hearts in it. Johnston the following week was in London, interviewing Lloyd George about the *Forward*.

Lloyd George showed him *The Worker*. " Look at this," he said, " I thought your paper was bad, but it's nothing to this. This can't be tolerated." The *Glasgow Times* had a paragraph commenting on the first issue, as follows:

" *The Worker* has appeared. It is presented as the organ of the Clyde Workers' Committee. Whoever has started the organ has pulled out all the stops and got both feet on the treadles."

We got out four issues and the fifth was on the press when the blow fell. In the fourth issue an article had appeared written by an I.L.P. pacifist entitled " Should the workers arm ? " and this was used as the pretext for attacking us.

Johnny Muir and I were arrested, as was also Walter Bell, manager of the S.L.P. Press. It was late on a cold winter night when we were thrown into the cells of the Northern police station.

After walking up and down for a while in my cell, I decided to settle down. There was no bed other than a composition block raised a little from the floor, shaped like a bed and pillow. I got my coat and jacket off, removed my shoes, pushed my feet into the sleeves of my jacket, put my hat beneath my head and covered myself with my overcoat. I soon got fairly comfortable and started counting

myself to sleep. Before I had succeeded I heard
footsteps coming along the corridor and then the
key going in the lock. The door was thrown open
by the turnkey and in walked John Wheatley
and Davy Kirkwood. I pulled on my shoes and
got up.

Kirkwood said, " Oh! my, what a business."
Wheatley asked the turnkey if there were no
blankets. He said there were, but he didn't advise
using them. They were lousy. Kirkwood said:
" My! oh my! " again. Wheatley asked me if I
was all right; when I assured him that I was, he
told me things weren't so good with Johnny. He
was very concerned about him. He told me he had
made arrangements to have us represented and we
should not worry.

It was my first time in prison and everything was
strange to me. I was so pleased with Wheatley's visit
that I was prepared to agree to anything. From that
time on, Wheatley's influence over several of the
comrades became so pronounced that they would
do nothing without consulting him.

He had engaged Rosslyn Mitchell, the solicitor,
to take charge of our case. He was a dapper little
gentleman with a beaming, cultivated smile. Someone had told him that he resembled Lord Rosebery,
and he tried to live up to the part, with winged
collar, spats, and all.

In the morning we came before a magistrate, and
were handed over to the Sheriff who committed us
to prison pending our trial in the High Court. We

were charged with: " Having on or about January 29th at 50 Renfrew Street or elsewhere in Glasgow attempted to cause mutiny, sedition or disaffection among the civilian population, and to impede, delay and restrict the production of war material by producing, printing, publishing and circulating amongst workers in and around Glasgow engaged on war materials, a newspaper entitled *The Worker*."

But the morning when word of the arrests got around, was the start of an eruption on the Clyde. Several of the factories " downed tools " and there was a demonstration at the Sheriff's Court. Kirkwood was with Wheatley at the court, but none of the Parkhead workers accompanied him. He did not try to bring them out as a demonstration, but came to the court with a promise to call them out if we were not liberated. Those who were already on strike were demanding our unconditional release, but Mr. Mitchell was already arranging for bail. The following morning, Wednesday, we were let out on bail of £50 each and those who had struck returned to work, leaving a feeling, not very pronounced, but nevertheless there—that Parkhead under Kirkwood's leadership had not played its part.

.   .   .   .   .

Some time before this, three dilution commissioners, Sir Thomas Munro, Lyndon Macassey and Isaac Mitchell, had come to Glasgow to introduce schemes of dilution in the factories. They had with them proposals, which meant not a limiting of the powers of the employers, but a serious limiting of the powers of the stewards. The Clyde Workers' Committee published a statement attacking these proposals. Then a delegate meeting came to the decision that no factory committee would have any dealings with the Commissioners, but would refer them to the Clyde Workers' Committee, which would meet them and discuss the Clyde as a whole.

The Commissioners felt their way around and soon realized what they were up against. After a week or two of vain endeavour, they concentrated their attention on Parkhead. We were seeing very little of Kirkwood at the time; he was almost always in the company of John Wheatley. A week after our liberation on bail, we met one night and were utterly staggered to learn that Parkhead had broken the front and signed a separate agreement with the Commissioners.

We sent for Kirkwood and found that it was only too true. He read out a statement he had submitted to the Commissioners, which was just a series of generalities, committing the Commissioners to nothing. But, tacked on to this, were the following clauses:

(1) That the income of the new class of labour be fixed, not on the sex, previous training or experience of the worker but upon the amount of work performed, based on rates presently obtaining for the particular operation.

(2) That a committee appointed by the workers be

accepted by the employers, with power to see that this arrangement is loyally carried out. Failing agreement between employer and the committee, the matter be referred to a final tribunal, mutually agreed.

(3) That a record of all past and present changes in practice be handed to the convenor of shop stewards and by him remitted to the District Office to be retained for future reference.

(4) That all skilled and semi-skilled men who were engaged at the Engineering trade in the service of the firm immediately prior to the war be granted a certificate to that effect.

(5) No alteration shall take place in this scheme unless and until due notice is given to the workmen concerned and the procedure is followed as prescribed by Clause 7 of Schedule 11, of the Munitions of War Act, 1915.

The fatal weakness was clauses one and two. Clause one refers only to payment according to output and clause two proposes a committee that *would meet the employers when any dispute on payments arose.*

There is no mention of any shop committee to regulate conditions or transfers in the various departments. With no provision made for such a shop committee, with the right to general supervision, obviously there was no provision for the chairman of such a committee or for the convenor of shop stewards supervising changes taking place, or intervening in particular departments where difficulties arose. All the employers were committed to was the retention of existing piece rates and the recognition of a committee on this question only

In the course of our talk with Kirkwood he declared he was concerned with Parkhead alone and as this agreement had safeguarded the Parkhead workers he was satisfied. This statement went circulating around the Clyde and caused incalculable harm. The whole front started cracking up. After they had got through in several places, the Commission came to the Albion. But our factory committee persuaded the management to dispense with the services of the Commission, claiming that we and they, the management, were quite capable of deciding what had to be done in such matters. The Commission were invited, very courteously of course, to leave the premises, after which the factory committee and the management worked out an agreement on the conditions under which the dilution would take place. This was a model agreement in the circumstances. All " Dilutees," women and men, would start at 30s. per week and in three equal monthly increases, would draw the full rate, with all bonuses, at the end of three months. Full inspection of conditions to be allowed to the factory committee with no interference or limitation in the ordinary functions of the committee.

Immediately this was signed, I went up to Barr and Stroud's, where Johnny Muir was employed, and gave him a copy. He was successful in getting the same agreement through there. Then, at Parkhead, things took an ugly turn. Hitherto it had been the custom for the convenor of shop stewards or chairman of the factory committee to go into any department where there was trouble, or for a representative of that department to visit the convenor. In Parkhead this had been the rule concerning Kirkwood for many years. Now, as a consequence of the agreement he himself had signed, he was prohibited from leaving his own department and no one was allowed to leave another department to see him, whatever the trouble might be. Each department was thus closed to its neighbours. Its troubles had to be settled without reference to the others.

When Kirkwood was presented with this ultimatum he resigned his position as convenor of shop stewards, declaring that he would never carry on under such conditions. The shop stewards decided not to accept his resignation and then, after fruitless negotiations with Sir William Beardmore, who simply referred them to the agreement, they called a strike. Immediately Kirkwood was arrested, so also were Messer, McManus, Bridges, Wainwright and several others. Tommy Clark was picked up a day or two later. They were taken to the station at night and entrained for Edinburgh and Aberdeen, deported from Glasgow. The following morning, the committee in the Albion decided to strike along with Parkhead and Dalmuir, the latter also a plant of Beardmore's. At Meechan's, a short way up the Clyde from the Albion, they were doing sub-contract work from Parkhead, and we succeeded in getting a stoppage there.

I rushed up to Barr and Stroud's to see Johnny

Muir. Barr and Stroud's hadn't stopped, neither had Weir's, Brown's, Fairfield's nor any other of the decisive factories. Parkhead had broken the front. Parkhead could take the consequences. Such was the situation we were facing.

When I saw Johnny he proposed we go into the city to see Wheatley. This we did, and out of our talk with him came the proposition that Johnny and I, in view of the fact that in the factories where we were employed full freedom of inspection was operating, should go to the Ministry of Munitions in London and make a fight to get this agreement made applicable all round, and the deportation order withdrawn.' This was considered more possible as Lloyd George was in France and Addison in charge of the Ministry. I saw the committee at the Albion and they supported this suggestion and promised whatever happened to hold the Albion out till we got back. We travelled down that night and, with the assistance of Ramsay MacDonald and Pringle (a Radical M.P.), an interview was arranged with Dr. Addison.

The day before, in an attack on the strike and in justification of the deportations, Addison had said in the House of Commons, " At different times strikes have been brought about sometimes on the most trivial grounds by a self-appointed body known as the Clyde Workers' Committee. This Committee decided about a fortnight ago to embark on a policy of holding up the production of the most important munitions of war in the Clyde district with the object, I am informed, of compelling the Government to repeal the Military Service Act, and the Munitions of War Act, and to withdraw all limitations on increases of wages and strike and all forms of Government control. . . . The Executive Committee of the Amalgamated Society of Engineers on the matter being reported to them by the local officials immediately issued a statement repudiating the strike, forbidding the payment of strike benefit and calling on the men to return to work."

Sir Edward Carson: " May I ask if it has been considered whether these men are not guilty of assisting the King's enemies and are thereby guilty of High Treason? "

Dr. Addison: " Yes. The whole matter is being considered." (*Hansard*, March 28, 1916.)

Sir Edward Carson, it should be mentioned here, was one of the members of the Government most anxious for a High Treason charge to be brought against the rebels of the Clyde. These were proletarian rebels, daring to oppose the high panjandrums of private property and robber imperialism. They were different entirely from the rebels of Ulster of whom, just two short years before, Carson himself had been the leader.

The Ulster rebels had been armed to the teeth, and threatened war against the Government if it dared to go ahead with its Home Rule for Ireland proposals. Carson and his associate, "Galloper" Smith, had uttered all kinds of violent incitement against the " Recognized and established Authorities," and actually succeeded in stirring up a mutiny of Army officers in the Curragh camp. I was living in Bangor (Ulster) in the early part of 1914, whence I travelled every morning to my work in Belfast.

One morning early, I turned into the Station Road, which ran up direct from the harbour. I found the road blocked with a detachment of Carson's " Private Army " with fixed bayonets. Nobody was allowed to enter the road. The " Storm Troops " were engaged in unloading a shipful of munitions, supplied by Germany.

Night after night the forces were out parading and drilling. In the factories and in other prominent places large, striking, proclamations were exhibited giving details of the signals that would be used to call a general uprising.

I remember another morning in February 1914. I came out of the station at Belfast and made my way along the docks to where I was employed. It was a raw cold morning. A heavy leaden sky blanketed Belfast with a steady penetrating drizzle of rain. As I approached the Liverpool dock, I found a great crowd gathering, many of them poorly clad, cold and shivering. They were waiting the arrival of the Liverpool boat and " the leader." I passed on my way to work, but later on in the day I read of the arrival and what happened.

When the boat drew in Carson did not disembark. Instead, Craig and some others drove up to the dock in their expensive cars. They went on board where breakfast had been prepared. They sat down in the comfort of the saloon and enjoyed it, while the hungry crowd clustered together for warmth outside. After their job of eating was finished they walked down the gangway amid the enthusiastic cheering of the rain-soaked crowd, entered the cars and drove off to Craigavon's Castle. The crowd dispersed, many of them making their way to the wretched Belfast slums they have to call homes.

But the remarkable thing about that visit was the character of the captions in the " Loyalist Press." It ran in great block letters:

" *He* IS WITH US TO-DAY."

" He " the great one, the saviour. Thus long before Hitler was heard of, the idea was already being operated in the North of Ireland. It is necessary to note this, to give particular attention to it especially on the part of those who say that " Britain is different," for it can be laid down with the utmost precision that there is nothing associated with fascism, its idea of centralization, its demagogy, its brutality or its independent army, that has not already been in evidence in this country.

In fact it is from the British bourgeoisie, farseeing and cunning, that most of the inspirations for the brutality of monopoly capitalism have come.

To revert to Addison. With the assistance of MacDonald and Pringle we kept at him, and latterly got him almost to the point of agreement on the

withdrawal of the deportation order. So near agreement were we that a meeting was fixed for the next
morning to decide on a formula. But the following
morning all went up in smoke. Lloyd George had
returned from France and when he heard what was
happening he nearly threw a fit. He ordered Addison to finish with the business. Addison obeyed and
sent a note to MacDonald ending our happy little
romance. In the afternoon in the House of Commons there was an awful blow-out arising from a
question put by Pringle asking why Addison had
broken off negotiations. Addison denied that there
had been " negotiations." There had been conver-
sations but no negotiations. Furthermore, Pringle
had come into Addison's private room without an
invitation. MacDonald had been welcome, but not
Pringle, he said. To which Pringle replied that I
had asked him to accompany us and had refused to
discuss anything unless he were present. This was
absolutely correct, as Pringle was outstanding in the
House of Commons as a critic of the Government.
Pringle put up a good defence, but was followed
by MacDonald who ruined his case and put him
at the mercy of Lloyd George and Addison.

In his most plaintive tones MacDonald bewailed
the fact that divisions had arisen between himself
and many of his old and valued friends in the House
of Commons. He then concluded, " But I beg this
House to believe me when I say that rather than
that division of opinion should make me an agent
to bring men out on strike just now I should wish

that something should happen of one kind or another which would destroy every particle of influence that ever I had with the working men of this country. Within two months of the outbreak of war I made publicly in my own constituency an appeal to men who are working on munitions to work honestly on munitions." (*Hansard*, March 30, 1916.)

This was meat and drink for the other fellows and they went all out against Pringle and the Clyde Workers' Committee.

Addison said of Pringle, " He has chosen to make himself the spokesman, in this House, of the Clyde Workers' Committee, a body which with a treacherous disregard of the highest National interests, has made itself responsible for promoting strife and putting obstacles in the way of the full and rapid equipment of our armies in the field." (*Hansard*, March 30, 1916.)

Lloyd George in a disconnected speech, " tore a passion to tatters." How he had listened and waited, he said, while Pringle spoke, for one word of the character which had later concluded the speech of his friend, the hon. member for Leicester (MacDonald). But not a word of condemnation for the strikers, only an attempt to justify them. And what was Pringle identifying himself with ? " This," he shouted, " is purely an organization for sedition, not merely against the Government but against the trade unions themselves."

To Pringle's taunt that he himself on a previous

occasion had testified to our sincerity, he said he
still held to that. What was all the trouble about
now? There would have been no trouble " had it
not been for this very sincere and rather fanatical
man coming to my friend, the hon. member for
Leicester. Had it not been for the fact that he
was sincere, and that therefore the men believed
in him, he could not have this influence for mis-
chief."

But let us give Lloyd George credit for being an
honest little fellow. He drew attention to the fact
that I was coming up for trial shortly and as the case
was *sub judice* he would not say anything to influence
it. Johnny Muir and I were sitting in the gallery;
and his touching impartiality almost brought tears to
our eyes.

When Johnny and I got back to Glasgow we
found things as we had left them. Parkhead was
still out, with only Dalmuir, Albion and Meechan's supporting them. It was clear that we were
in a hopeless position. Two days we had been away,
but these days were vital. In such a strike it is the
first days that count. If I had gone to see the factory
committees at several of the other factories, instead
of trying a piece of " clever " intriguing in London,
the situation might have been saved. But now it
was too late. There was no chance now of getting
any others to act. Our visit to London at such a
critical moment was evidence of the demoralization that had spread amongst us, with the rapid
offensive that had taken place. We had not pre-

pared ourselves for it; and when it came we collapsed. The strike continued for several days; then one morning, while we were still out at the Albion, word came that Parkhead were back in. The demoralization was complete.

CHAPTER VII

CONSCRIPTION AND PRISON

DURING all this period the general campaign against the war was proceeding more actively than ever. McLean was everywhere. His indoor meetings were packed out, with crowds outside clamouring for admission; until he was forced to run two meetings a night. He was the centre of the anti-war movement; and all the other movements, whatever their tendencies, supported the general line he was taking. He demanded an immediate armistice, with no annexations and no indemnities; along with this went his drive for the revolutionary overthrow of the capitalist class.

But the sinister campaign for conscription was growing, and already, by the end of 1915, had reached the stage of definite proposals. Therefore, all kinds of people were looking to the Clyde for some action to prevent it. Early in January 1916, Bruce Glasier came to Glasgow and had a meeting at the Glasgow headquarters of the I.L.P., with the leaders of the Clyde Workers' Committee. He begged us to do something to stop conscription. Others came with similar appeals, to all of which we answered that we were prepared to do all in our power to bring the war to an end and to defeat the capitalist class.

At the beginning of January we passed a resolution and circulated it widely throughout the Clyde. It read as follows:

" This delegate meeting of the Clyde Workers' Committee, recognizing that the purport of the conscription is not a fuller supply of soldiers but the cheapening of soldiers and the military control of industry and consequently the abolition of the function of our trade unions, resolves to take such action as is necessary to prevent conscription."

In the first issue of *The Worker* we made this a feature. We carried on the agitation in the factories, while McLean conducted it outside. Every day he spoke at the factory gates. From one end of the Clyde to the other he travelled. Every night he spoke on the streets, in the halls or lecture rooms. He was turning out scores of new agitators and distributing them to all parts of the area. All over the Clyde the atmosphere was becoming electrical. We should have realized that the situation was now so full of danger for the Government, and for " the successful prosecution of the war," that they would be forced to take action.

But while McLean's personality carried us all forward into a torrent of agitation, and while through the factory committees and the Clyde Workers' Central Committee, we had a strong workshop organization, there was no experienced political leadership that could harmonize all these currents and weld them into a whole. So when the attack came, we could not meet it.

On Sunday, February 6, McLean was arrested by the military authorities and confined to Edinburgh Castle. But there he caused so much trouble that they gladly handed him over to the civil authorities, who, after committing him for trial on a charge of sedition, allowed him out on a bail of £100. Petrov was interned, and after the revolution, deported to Russia. Maxton, McDougall and Jack Smith—the latter an English anarchist who had been work-in the Clyde engineering shops for a few years—were also arrested on charges of sedition.

Maxton and McDougall, it may be said, had deliberately set out to get arrested, as an alternative to being conscripted; this in itself was an indication of the lack of political understanding and leadership existing at the time. Edinburgh was fixed as the venue for the various sedition trials. This made it bad for us, as Edinburgh, while having a considerable working-class population, was by tradition aristocratic and reactionary. But to make things a thousand times worse there was a Zeppelin raid over Edinburgh with considerable casualties and damage just a few days before the trials opened. We were accused in the Press of being in the pay of the Germans. " German gold," according to the patriots, was pouring into the Clyde. We had even " received a letter from the Kaiser thanking us for our co-operation." The " letter " was actually in existence in the form of a leaflet, but it didn't come from Germany; it was manufactured in Whitehall.

But whether or no the Kaiser thanked us for our co-operation, we certainly couldn't thank the Germans for their co-operation, for that air raid in Edinburgh eliminated every spark of sympathy for the " German agents " of the Clyde, from the minds and hearts of the twelve good men and true, and left them stony-eyed and stony-hearted, with a verdict of " guilty " sewed up tight before the cases started.

Eventually, McLean came up for trial. Many workers had come up from Glasgow and some of them had succeeded in getting into the court. The atmosphere in Edinburgh was hostile; in the court it was deadly. Lord Strathclyde occupied the bench and his attitude was that to be expected. The case against McLean was put by the Lord Advocate, Avon Clyde, with a number of police agents giving evidence. McLean defended himself, and never did he rise to greater heights. In the midst of enemies and informers, he lashed out and seared them with his contempt. This speech from the dock, later published as a pamphlet, was full of striking phrases. " I stand here not as the accused," he declared, " but as the accuser, the accuser of capitalism dripping with blood from head to foot."

He declared his revolutionary faith, his hatred of capitalism and the predatory wars of capitalism, his undying loyalty to the class war—the war of the workers. It was a magnificent effort, during which the judge and Lord Advocate sat glum and glaring. After the judge's summing up no time was lost in getting a verdict of "guilty". McLean was sentenced to three years' penal servitude.

The next trial was that of Muir, Walter Bell and myself. We came up in the same court, but what a contrast! If McLean held high the banner of revolutionary struggle, we dragged it, or allowed it to be dragged, in the mire. Even now it is hard to think of it without a feeling of shame. Wheatley was there all the time, advising us; the impeccable Mitchell, our solicitor; and a counsel, of whom we had never heard before and have never heard of since.

They tried to persuade me to keep out of the witness box, arguing that the prosecution had no direct evidence of responsibility, which they would endeavour to get if anyone went into the box; as they might try to force me to tell who wrote the article. But, despite all their efforts to dissuade me, I took the stand. One of the exhibits in the case was our first leaflet, in which we accused the trade union leaders of treachery by supporting the Government.

Did I accept responsibility for this leaflet? Yes. Had I written the article in *The Worker*? No. Who wrote it? I didn't know. Do you approve of the editor putting it in the paper? Yes. Thus the questions and answers went on until it was obvious we were well sunk. Every time the Lord Advocate made a point, he smirked at the judge and jury. Of course, it would have made no difference as regards the final decision. Even if I had not gone into the box, our conviction was assured from the beginning; but Mitchell had been trying to persuade us that our penalty might only be a fine, a heavy fine perhaps, but no more. It was a rotten business all through, and my only satisfaction was that, as a result of going into the box, I was able to share responsibility with Johnny Muir.

This trial—and the subsequent trial of Maxton, Smith and McDougall, which followed the same lines—was another example of the lack of experience and leadership, capable of a policy that would cover such a situation and provide those involved with the necessary guidance in carrying through a working-class fight. It is useless making excuses now, however. The conduct of both cases, following the stirring example of McLean, was a disgrace to the movement. If we had made a fight, just because of the weak case against us there was a faint possibility that we might have made it difficult for them to sentence us, because of the feeling we could have aroused among the workers. But our capitulation simply played into their hands. Weakness and timidity can avail us nothing in such a situation. The heroic conduct of Dimitrov when faced by Nazi hangmen, has shown to all workers the value of a courageous stand under such circumstances, however perilous.

After the verdict of " guilty," the court was

adjourned until the following day. When we were brought up next morning, Muir and I were sentenced to twelve months' imprisonment, while Walter Bell was sentenced to three months. A week later, Maxton and McDougall got similar sentences. Jack Smith got an extra six months for being in possession of a bundle of revolutionary literature when arrested.

So ended for the time being the revolt on the Clyde. With John McLean, the leader of anti-war activity, in jail, and the leaders of the shop stewards deported or imprisoned, the movement fell into the hands of some S.L.P. sectarians, who stifled all possible expression of a fighting character. They started the W.I.I.U. (Workers' International Industrial Union) or rather, as it was already in existence in a small way, they seized the opportunity provided by the general breakdown to extend it widely in the factories. They were against strikes for " reforms," they were for " educating " the workers; and then, when they were all educated and class-conscious, instead of striking, instead of walking out of the factories, they would " take and hold." But no fight against the war, no strikes, just " educate " the workers—the " education " consisting of doctrinaire recitation, and then, one day, as a consequence, we'd " take and hold."

.   .   .   .   .

Now that we were in prison, the influence of the peculiar Mr. Petrov began to manifest itself on

McLean and McDougall. We all went to Calton Jail, McLean only for a couple of weeks, before being transferred to Peterhead convict prison. Calton Jail, which has now been pulled down, was opened in 1816. It was easily the worst prison in the country. Cold, silent and repellent, the discipline was brutal and the diet atrocious. There was no "association" labour, most of the prisoners working in their cells at mat-making and similar occupations. The one-hour's exercise in the morning was the only opportunity they had of seeing each other, when desperate attempts were made to exchange a whisper or two.

For breakfast we had thick porridge and sour milk; for dinner, soup and a piece of dry bread; and for supper thick porridge and sour milk. It was a harsh change, and it took us a few days to get accustomed to it. But with McLean and McDougall, the one in Peterhead and the other in Calton, things began to go badly. Petrov's insistent whispering began to have its effect. All the time he was in Glasgow he had been hissing into their ears—spies, spies everywhere. In prison, torture. Warders at the cell doors during the night, jeering at the prisoner; poison in the food; sly questions with a barbed point in them, like, "How's your health to-day?" This with a laugh, to let the prisoner know that the questioner was aware that his health was failing.

He kept at them until he had them dodging around corners and then squinting round again to see who was after them. We used to laugh with John about it, but in prison it was no laughing matter. So affected had they been by Petrov that in their different prisons they had the same illusions —the prison officials were trying to destroy their health and their sanity.

One Sunday morning, after we had been in about six weeks, we were marched to the chapel as usual. We were all seated waiting the entry of the chaplain. As he came in and approached the pulpit, McDougall stood up and shouted, " Sir, I want you to write to my father. The warders are talking in my door at night trying to drive me insane." Two warders led him out of the chapel and returned him to his cell. Later on that day he had a terrible attack of nerves. I rang for the warder on duty and asked him to let me along to calm him down, but he couldn't do anything as he was on duty by himself, the others of the short-handed laundry staff being away at dinner.

It was a heartbreaking experience to sit there and listen to him and be unable to do anything. Of course there was nobody talking at his cell door at night. The warders all went home after the prisoners were in bed, except for the man on duty at the gate house, and only a night watchman in soft-soled sneakers made his regular rounds at night. Anyone who has been in prison will understand that it is not possible to talk in any part of the hall without the sound of the voices being heard in every cell. Maxton was in the next cell to me, and at

" nine o'clock bell " (bed-time) I made a practice
of playing the verse of the " Red Flag" by tapping
on the wall, while Maxton contributed the chorus;
after which I gave what was supposed to be a
rendering of " Hip, hip, hurrah! " This went on
for a month or so, till a prisoner up above put in a
complaint about noisy neighbours, and Maxton
was removed to another cell.

The day following his breakdown McDougall
was transferred to Perth for special care and attention. In the meantime, in Peterhead, McLean was
imagining similar things, warders at his door at
midnight, and interference with his food. When
after our liberation we met again I tried in every
way to disabuse their minds of these illusions, but
could not make any impression on them.

Following the McDougall affair, some questions
were asked in Parliament about conditions in Calton
Jail, and it was decided that certain officials together
with a representative of Labour should make a visit
to the prison. We knew nothing about this, of
course. I was quite surprised, therefore, to have my
door opened one day while I was sitting at dinner,
and to find myself confronted by a very imposing
deputation. Some gentlemen from the Home
Office, the chief warder said, had come to see how I
was getting on.

I was immediately on my guard. Not for all the
world was I going to let the authorities think that
I was the least bit upset at being in prison. How
did I like my work? As it happened, there was a

small engineering shop with a very capable engineer warder in charge. He was responsible for all repair work in the prison. I got handed over to this warder and spent my time going around from one part of the prison to another. I talked to warders, and I talked to prisoners. Periodically I got a visit up to where Maxton was working and spent a short time chatting with him. Often, especially on a Saturday, when I overhauled the cell lights, I was able to get a few words with Johnny Muir. So when asked how I liked my work, I said it was all right. I had been in many worse jobs and added if I could get out at night I would stick it long enough. The chief warder said: " You wouldn't go out with those clothes on? " " Try me and see," I said.

It wasn't till long after that I learned that there was a Labour man, David Lowe, along with the officials, supposedly looking for some faults in the prison system. If any of us had been asked about these we could have given plenty. Later on I got many opportunities to do so. Dr. Devon, the Prison Commissioner, came into the prison very often. Always he sent for me to have a talk about conditions and about how the system could be improved. The new prison at Saughton, while it is still a prison and therefore to be avoided, is a striking contrast to what the Calton was, and is mainly due to the work of Devon.

I succeeded in carrying on a certain amount of propaganda amongst the warders, especially against bullying of the prisoners, something we had never stood for in the workshops. As a consequence of this, the day before my liberation, the chaplain, Dr. John White, came to see me. We had many quarrels on politics and religion, but he always came back for more. But this day he said, " Well, you're going to leave us."

" Yes," I replied. " To-morrow morning."

" Well, Gallacher," he said, " believe me, I'm sorry, for you have raised very considerably the moral tone of this prison." I hadn't noticed it myself, but that was the reverend gentleman's opinion.

When I returned to the same prison two and a half years later, a group of warders headed by the chief warder met me at the door. The chief stepped forward and held out his hand as he said, " Well, it's an old friend back again." All the others followed suit, so I was welcomed " home."

·   ·   ·   ·   ·

While we were wearing out our days in prison, the deportees were making the best of a somewhat dull life in Edinburgh. Funds there were in plenty. Thousands of pounds had been raised to maintain the deportees and the dependents of the prisoners. John Wheatley and two other comrades were appointed trustees of the fund and allocated support in a somewhat arbitrary manner. Wheatley was especially interested in Kirkwood. Beardmore's works at Parkhead was a gigantic concern employing many thousands of men. It bordered on

Shettleston, where Wheatley was parliamentary candidate and where he and Kirkwood both lived. Wheatley was determined to exploit Kirkwood and the Parkhead situation to the full. In 1916 conscription was in full swing, and the deportees were faced with the necessity of getting employment or of being conscripted. They weren't allowed to work in Edinburgh, but they were in a position where they could leave Edinburgh to seek for work, provided they travelled farther away from Glasgow. After serious consideration they decided to go to Liverpool. When Wheatley heard of this, he hurried through to Edinburgh, and persuaded Kirkwood to let McManus, Messer and the others go to Liverpool, but to remain in Edinburgh himself. As Kirkwood was over military age, he wasn't affected by the need for getting a job, and there was sufficient money to maintain him in Edinburgh. Kirkwood was easily persuaded, so the others went off and left him in his solitary grandeur.

From then on the situation was completely in Wheatley's hands. In Liverpool, McManus, Messer and the others encountered every kind of difficulty. They had to pawn everything they had to keep going, but they could get nothing from the fund. They were no longer deportees, so Wheatley decided. There was now only one deportee, Kirkwood. The whole apparatus of the I.L.P., including *Forward* was brought into play to boost him. Soon all others were forgotten; Kirkwood, *the* deportee was established.

Whoever went from Glasgow, or in fact, from any other part of the country, to Edinburgh, Wheatley saw to it that he or she visited Kirkwood. Not only so, but he kept up a continuous series of arranged visits at the week-ends.

The great event, however, was the appearance of Kirkwood as a delegate to the Manchester Labour Party Conference, which opened on Tuesday, January 23, 1917. In the Wednesday Session Kirkwood stepped on to the platform to second a resolution moved by W. H. Hutchinson, of the A.E.U., on the restoration of trade union rights. He got a great reception. After a few words about the resolution he read out a carefully prepared statement on the deportations. After sketching the developments of the trouble leading up to the deportations, he went on to say that the Government after keeping them in banishment for nine months, now proposed to allow them to return home if they signed a document promising to work loyally and faithfully, *and behave obediently to their trade unions.* He claimed he had always done this. He was no criminal, so why should he be asked to sign this humiliating and degrading document. There was one reason and one reason only, and that was to whitewash his persecutors. Then with great dramatic power he declared, " I tell this conference I am finished with deportation. I go back to my home in Glasgow or to jail."

As one man, the delegates jumped to their feet. They waved their papers and cheered again and again. Then came loud and angry shouts for Arthur Henderson, who was obviously one of those referred to as " persecutors." John Scurr, writing of the scene, in the *Herald* of January 27, says: " Fierce emotions showed themselves, and the call for Henderson at the close was like the snarl of an angry beast."

Henderson took the platform, white-faced and nervous, but his cunning had not deserted him. He made all kinds of specious excuses for his own conduct and then demanded a special committee to inquire into the whole matter. This was a master stroke as it at once took attention away from the immediate consideration of the issue and got it relegated to a future so pregnant with changing events as to guarantee the quiet burial of this dangerous episode. After some more or less spasmodic inquiries it got buried all right, but one thing that couldn't be buried was the following letter written by Henderson to a correspondent in Glasgow:

1 Victoria Street,
London, S.W.
April 5, 1916.

Dear Mr. McLeod,

I beg to acknowledge receipt of your favour of the 1st, and note your observations with regard to the position on the Clyde. I do not think you over-estimate the danger of the situation, or that you exaggerate the incitement that has been used by men of self-imposed leadership. There is but one of your statements I doubt, as to further appeals being made to the patriotism of the men concerned. They have been appealed to by their own trade union leaders and by Cabinet Ministers, but they appear determined to take their own course no matter what is said. It remains to be seen how the stern enforcement of the law, such as the transfer of the ringleaders from the affected area will assist.

Yours sincerely,

ARTHUR HENDERSON.

All efforts at whitewashing failed to deceive the Glasgow workers. They knew only too well the part Henderson had played as one of Lloyd George's fuglemen and so Glasgow was a " banned " area for Henderson. In 1928, escorted by no others than Kirkwood and Wheatley he attempted a public meeting in Shettleston and there was a " near riot " as a consequence, with about ten or a dozen of us arrested by the specially mobilized police who were held in readiness at the hall.

But to get back to the " deportee." It may be asked, why hadn't the question of a return to Glasgow been considered from the first days of the deportation ? To this I can only answer that we had been so accustomed to " legality " that when the shock measures of the Government came we were quite unprepared for them. We were " legal " revolutionaries. But here at Manchester a declaration of war had been made. To every part of the country, delegates returned and told the stirring story of Kirkwood, the deportee, " I'm going back to my home in Glasgow or to jail."

Yet long before the first delegate reported, the "revolt" was ended and Kirkwood was back in Edinburgh giving an admirable example of how a well-behaved deportee should conduct himself.

On the Friday night he left the conference and returned very quietly to Glasgow. Only a few of his immediate friends, plus the police, knew he was there. On the Sunday he was visited by two special officers who talked very courteously with him and proposed once again the signing of the document. On his refusal they left without giving any indication of what would happen next. On the Tuesday he went to Crieff for a holiday and rest, and there the following day, Wednesday, he was arrested and taken back to Edinburgh. When they arrived at Edinburgh, he was taken to the Castle where he was confined until the Friday, when he was liberated on his promise not to return to Glasgow, without the permission of the Competent Military Authority, Colonel Levita. Arrangements were then made for him to go for a rest to the Moffat Hydropathic, while an agitation was conducted in Glasgow to get the deportation order withdrawn.

In the Calton Jail, Johnnie Muir and Maxton were having a rough time. The confinement and conditions were telling on their health. Maxton never was very strong at the best, and the diet, apart from anything else, was enough to knock the knees from anyone. But Johnny, gentle and sensitive, was paying a terrible price. Every chance

I got I talked to him and tried to cheer him up. It used to be pathetic to see him try to smile when I worked off some humorous story.

At this time also we had in prison with us a large number of conscientious objectors. It was an awful experience for them. One young student named Fraser, in the course of a talk I had with him, was very distressed.

"Keep your chin up," I said, "it'll pass and you'll be laughing about it one day."

"But it's so awful," he said, "to be in here, and for doing nothing."

"Well," I answered him, "surely it's better to be in for doing nothing than to be in for doing something."

"I never thought of it that way," he replied.

On Saturday, February 3, 1917, Maxton and McDougall were released, and then on the 13th of the same month, Muir and I came out. Instead of being liberated from Edinburgh, Muir and I were taken quietly to Glasgow the afternoon before our liberation and locked up in Duke Street prison for the night, from where we were let out early in the morning. Only a very few got to know about this, and only at the last moment. Amongst them was John Wheatley. He met us and told us he had made all arrangements for us to go off for a holiday. Kirkwood, he informed us, was at Moffat Hydropathic, and we had to join him there. On Wednesday we travelled to Moffat, Muir and his fiancée, Maxton and McDougall, myself and my wife.

Kirkwood met us at Moffat station and then paraded us on our way out to the Hydro. It was a huge building, with extensive grounds. The whole place was furnished and decorated without regard to cost. But it was practically empty. The war had denuded it of patrons, and except for ourselves and a shell-shocked officer, who had become a dipsomaniac, it was untenanted. There was quite a number of attendants and they were all at Kirkwood's beck and call. He gathered them together like an ancient squire and introduced his guests. We had to have every attention. He knew they would look after us as they were looking after him—all done in the grand manner. We were shown to our rooms, introduced to the sprays, the masseur, and the swimming pool. It was some place!

In the evening we were talking in a large and very comfortable sitting-room. In wandered the " dipsomaniac." He and I had already had a friendly chat. He came over and sat beside me on the couch, while Kirkwood glared at him. He wanted to tell me some " hair-raising " stories about the engineers and the miners and how they were traitors to the country. I sat and joked with him. He was such an unfortunate wreck. But Kirkwood got up and went out. A few minutes later he returned with the manager, who came over and invited the officer to leave.

I said, " But he's all right; he isn't doing any harm."

The manager replied, " This is Mr. Kirkwood's private room and only his guests can come in."

The war casualty went away, a sad and melancholy sight. I turned on Kirkwood, " You had no right to do that; the poor fellow wasn't doing any harm."

" Nobody can insult my class," he declared, as though addressing a mass meeting. " Nobody can insult my class and remain in my company." I winked at the others and let the matter drop.

On the Friday night we were in the same private sitting-room when a bill was handed to Kirkwood. I nearly collapsed when I saw it. It represented a full week for Kirkwood, but for the rest of us from Wednesday afternoon till Friday—and it amounted to £30. I said, " That's terrible. It's simply throwing money away." Davy said it was all right. There was a good bit of money left in the funds so there was nothing to worry about. But I drew his attention to the fact that it was ordinary working men and women who were subscribing to the fund and if he was so concerned about the people of his class he wouldn't waste their money getting away from them.

" At any rate," I said, " I'm finished. I pack up to-morrow and clear out of here for good."

We had a reception to attend in Glasgow on Saturday and arrangements had been made for us to return to Moffat and continue our holiday. My strong objections to the Hydro affected the others and our discussion ended with Muir, Maxton and McDougall falling into line with me.

The next morning we left Moffat Hydro with Davy remaining as the solitary representative of his class, ready with the assistance of the manager to defend his class against the forlorn and neglected dipsomaniac.

.   .   .   .   .

The short holiday over, we were now faced with the necessity for picking up the threads and fitting into the struggle once again. While there had been a considerable slackening in factory activity, the general campaign against the war was being assiduously carried on. Not only was there a continuous flood of propaganda meetings, but many conferences were being held also, involving representatives from trade union branches and various political and peace organizations, all concerned with some phase of anti-war activity.

But the big question now that we were released, was the continued imprisonment of McLean. After the first shock of the collapse in 1916 had been got over an agitation was started for the release of the prisoners, directed especially against the savage sentence passed on McLean.

The week following our liberation a great mass meeting was held in St. Mungo Hall to give us a welcome back. The hall was packed to suffocation with a mass of active workers drawn from all over the Clyde. When the platform party, which included Muir,

Maxton, McDougall, and myself came on there was an extraordinary scene of wild enthusiasm. The spirit of fight was alive and was clearly expressing itself.

I was first speaker, and I remember relating a recurrent incident of my travels to Manchester as an executive member of the union. Four of us went each month for a week-end executive meeting —Sam Nimlin, the organizer, " Jock " Stewart of Cathcart, myself, and another who came from Greenock. This Greenock comrade always arrived at the train in Central Station just a short time before it started. The other three of us reserved him a corner seat. He usually had a drink or two before arriving and as a consequence was always in a jovial mood. He would step in, take his corner seat, beam at the rest of us and then favour us with the solitary line of a song. Whether he knew more of it I never learned, but on every occasion we got the one line.

" I'll give it to you," I told the meeting, " as he gave it to us "—" Here we are again, boys, here we are again."

This started the meeting off on a good note, and then when I and the subsequent speakers declared for all our forces being brought into the fight to release John McLean, the roof was nearly lifted off the building. " All in favour of the fight to release McLean?" A sea of hands. "Good! Now into the factories with the agitation and rouse the workers as they've never been roused before. McLean must be released."

Soon the Government had to take note of the fact that the "unrest" on the Clyde was assuming serious proportions once again, and that the centre of the trouble was the continued imprisonment of McLean. Hints began to be dropped of his probable early release and before very long he was transferred from Peterhead Prison to Perth; a very significant step for the authorities to take. But there was no slackening of the campaign. On the contrary, we threw greater energy into it than ever before.

One of the most potent factors in the revival was the February Revolution in Russia. "Free Russia" was emblazoned on our banners and mighty demonstrations in support of the revolution were organized all over Scotland.

A Russian warship was lying in the Clyde at the time, and we invited the officers and crew up to meet us in the International Hall on the South side of Glasgow. Night after night they were there with us rejoicing in the great news from Russia, although some of the officers didn't appear to be too enthusiastic about the strength and activity of the ship's committee.

But the association with the revolutionary sailors and the attitude of several of the officers soon made it clear to us that the revolution still had a long way to travel, that heavy struggles still lay before the Russian proletariat. Therefore while we welcomed and were inspired by " Free Russia " we understood that " Free Russia " could only remain free if the workers succeeded in getting and maintaining power.

Here we were in the early months of 1917 with the great masses of Glasgow aroused to the highest pitch of enthusiasm. " Release McLean," " Long Live Free Russia," " Down with War—Down with the Warmakers." How is it possible to describe now those hectic days and the never-ending stream of activity that was carried on?

In the midst of it all were the sectarians, who, still wedded to their shibboleths, sneered at everything and tried to instil the deadly virus of passivity by means of their " magic key "—" Wait till the workers are class-conscious, then we'll take and hold." With the breakdown of the movement they had penetrated the factories, had almost paralysed the factory organization. We knew something like this had been going on, but never dreamed things were as bad as they actually were.

The first difficulty we met was that while Johnny Muir was given his job back in Barr and Stroud's, I was given my books at the Albion with a sort of an apology from the manager that he wasn't in a position to restart me. I then learned to my great disgust that the Ministry of Munitions had barred me from the large factories; the only job I would be allowed to take was in one of the several small places where only three or four men were employed.

The following quotation from the second volume of Lloyd George's *War Memoirs* makes quite clear now what was behind the Ministry's attitude at that time. Speaking of his visit to Clyde, he says of Kirkwood that " despite a theatrical frown he was fundamentally easy to get on with." This is followed by a reference to Tommy Clark as a " natural savage," then he adds:

" Later on I met Mr. Gallacher, a Communist, whose manners were quite perfect, and whose tones were soft, but he left no doubt in my mind that his was the most sinister influence."

I got started in a little shop off St. Vincent Street, a branch of Robinson's of Liverpool, ship telegraph manufacturers. It was a useful job in one way, as it brought me into touch with the naval department, and through a friend there I got an official letter informing all and sundry that I was engaged on Admiralty business and should not be hindered in any way. This enabled me to make contacts in many places, especially in Rosyth where we managed to get all kinds of literature conveyed and distributed. Had the authorities known I was carrying such a letter there would have been real trouble in the department, but I had sufficient regard for the friend to make only the most careful use of it.

Once started, we called for a meeting of shop stewards to be held in the Ingram Street Hall. Messer and McManus were still in Liverpool, Tommy Clark in Aberdeen, and Kirkwood at Moffat Hydro, so we were a much depleted leadership. I prepared a document dealing with immedi-

ate activities and organisational measures requisite
to their accomplishment. The small hall we had
taken was filled to capacity—about one hundred
were present when the meeting opened.

When I had made my statement and submitted
my proposals, I was subjected to an immediate and
terrific barrage, led by T. L. Smith and his friend,
Ness, the shell-backed sectarian leaders of the
W.I.I.U. They said I had come back to a new
Clyde, a Clyde that had learned something while
I was away. No more " wild adventures," no more
wasted effort, but a steady development of class-
conscious education until we had a class-conscious
organization that would " take and hold."

I tried my best to stem the tide of opposition they
had let loose but failed completely. After I had
been attacked and battered from side to side, Smith
got up and said: " You're finished, you and your
policy of perpetual strikes. Now we'll leave you."
Then in a louder voice, " All members of the
W.I.I.U. will leave this meeting." I was staggered
when practically the whole meeting filed out.
Seven of us were left. One of the seven was the
present Glasgow District Secretary of the A.E.U.,
Brother Fyffe, a comrade who has proved his
devotion and loyalty to the movement on many
occasions.

For a few moments we gazed at each other almost
in a state of suspended animation. Then I said:
" Well, it looks like we've got a lot of work to do."
Will Fyffe said, " Aye, it does that."

I then made some suggestions as to what I thought should be done and turning to Johnny Muir asked him what he thought about them.

" I don't know," he replied, " I'd like to consult Wheatley."

I said, " For Christ's sake, Johnny, what's the matter with you? "

He answered very quietly and sadly: " I don't know. I don't feel up to it."

" Aw, pull yourself together," I said. " You'll soon be all right again."

But it was no use. There was something wrong with Johnny. It had been noticeable at the St. Mungo Hall meeting. Something had gone out fo him, something vital, making him just a shadow of what he had been. It had a somewhat depressing effect on us. Johnny Muir, in many respects our ablest and most valuable comrade, with his spirit crushed by the refined torture of the British prison system! It was tragic.

From that time on Johnny Muir never moved apart from Wheatley.* Wheatley, strong, resolute and dominant, might have become a colossal figure if he had devoted himself to a study of Marxism

* Johnny became a member of the I.L.P. and as their nominee won Maryhill for Labour in 1922. He was given a minor post in the First Labour Government, 1924. But he was never able to overcome the effects of his harsh experiences in Calton Jail. He died in his early forties.

" Lo, some we loved, the fairest and the best,
    That time and fate from out their vintage press'd
        Have drunk their cup a round or two before
    And one by one crept silently to rest."

and revolutionary politics instead of intrigue. He was the only one of the outstanding Labour leaders who participated in any way in our activities, always of course from the outside. But if ever he was wanted for advice, encouragement or help of any kind, his services were at our disposal day or night. Often we turned to him and made use of his services, but all the time we had to take care he didn't simply swallow us up.

There we were then, seven of us, Johnny Muir, because of his health, quite unable to carry on. Not only was a terrific campaign being fought all over the area against the war and for the release of McLean, centred on the preparations for May Day, but a big issue had arisen between the Government and the unions on the question of " payment by results." Of course, a measure of piecework, or bonus, had always operated in various shops throughout the Clyde, but always the basic rate had been protected. Proposals were now put forward to make " payment by results " general. I was still attending the official meetings of the Allied Trades and we had many heated discussions on this question. I got a proposal accepted by the Allied Trades that was later presented to the Government officials, expressing the attitude of the trades unions as a whole that " piecework prices be decided by the workers in the factories, through their own factory committees, and that any objection on the part of the employers to the prices proposed, be submitted to the munitions department, but in the meantime and pending the hearing of the employers' appeal, the proposed price to operate in the factory."

This proposal put the unions in a very strong, in fact an invulnerable position for the fight against the Government, and also aroused the greatest interest and discussion in the factories. In such a situation, it was obvious it was only a matter of time, and a very short time, provided we gave adequate attention to the job, until we had the workshop movement vigorous and advancing once again.

As a matter of fact, by the beginning of May, we were in a position to say we had broken through the sectarian wall of the W.I.I.U., and had made a real advance towards the penetration of the factories. This advance was undoubtedly made possible by the intense campaign that was sweeping the Clyde for a revolutionary celebration on May 6, the first Sunday in May. From before the war, we had maintained a continuous campaign for the celebration on May 1, and there is no doubt that but for the arrests and deportations, which took away all the principal advocates of the First of May, the decision in 1917 would have been to hold the demonstration on May 1. The May Day Committee, however, had already, at the beginning of the year, made its decision and issued the invitations to the unions for May 6, so we could do nothing to alter the date; but we threw all our energy into making it an expression of revolutionary solidarity with the workers of " Free Russia," and with the workers of all other lands.

Never had there been such a May Day demonstration as Glasgow witnessed that Sunday. It was estimated that between seventy and eighty thousand people marched in the procession itself, while about a quarter of a million lined the streets. Bands and banners, slogans and streamers, singing and cheering, all contributed towards a scene of mass enthusiasm. Around the many platforms on Glasgow Green, the resolutions and speeches were cheered again and again. Along with the resolution declaring our solidarity with the Soviets of workers', peasants' and soldiers' delegates, we passed a resolution which read, " The demonstration declares for the overthrow of the capitalist system of production for profit. . . . Sends its fraternal greetings to the workers of all lands. . . . And in the interests of the solidarity of labour, *we hereby declare in favour of the 1st of May being held as a general holiday.*"

Glasgow was stirred to its depths that first Sunday of May; but it was necessary to carry the revolutionary feeling into the factories and get the factories into line with the general mood. We therefore called a further meeting of factory representatives for Sunday afternoon, May 13. On this occasion we had made much better preparations than for our earlier effort. Furthermore, the " comb-out " proposals of the Government were creating considerable agitation throughout England and there were continual threats of strike action in a number of the English engineering districts. A considerable shop stewards' movement was already operating in Sheffield, and a meeting had been held on April 29 to set up a factory organization for the London area.

The fellow who coined the slogan " Kitchener wants you " was credited with having hit on a brilliant idea; but whoever coined the " comb-out " phrase couldn't have thought of a worse one from the point of view of the war-makers. All those engineering workers whose places could be taken by women or by men unfit for active service had to be taken out of the factories and pushed into the army. It was in connection with the attempt to do this that the unhappy term " comb-out " was used. The engineers were being treated as " lice," and the most violent indignation was aroused everywhere as a consequence.

It was with rumours of all kinds coming from England that preparations were made for the meeting of factories' representatives on the afternoon of Sunday, 13. In addition to this meeting a great mass demonstration was being organized for the same evening in St. Andrew's Hall, to celebrate the Russian Revolution. Bob Smillie, Ramsay MacDonald and several others were billed to speak and it was obvious the hall would never hold the crowd that would come. Several of us had to take responsibility for organizing the demonstration and ensuring that the outside, or overflow demonstration was effectively handled.

Then on the Sunday afternoon, when the factory

delegates met, we had to face the fact not of rumours, but of an actual strike affecting London, Birmingham, Coventry and Manchester. The exact proportions of the strike were not known, but it was clear that strikes had broken out in all these areas. We had a good representation from the factories at this meeting, most of the representatives having got over their period of " Left-sickness," and although a number still clung to the " Take and hold " abortion, the majority were for getting on with the struggle in the factories. But the " sectarianism " of the past period had driven many of the official shop stewards out of the factory committee movement and thus caused a considerable division in some of the shops with a consequent serious weakening of the movement.

One big problem was how to overcome this and bring back into the movement all those shop stewards who were now merely acting in the formal character of " pence-card " stewards. But even as we considered this, we had to face the fact that strike action was developing in England and that we had to do everything possible to prepare the Clyde to take supporting action. It was decided I should leave Glasgow that night after the demonstration and travel down to London: from there, go to Birmingham, Coventry, Sheffield and Manchester, making contact with the shop stewards: and then report to a special meeting on Wednesday night the 16th. Meanwhile, the delegates would sound the feeling in the shops.

The evening demonstration was tremendous. Long before the advertised time great crowds were lined up all through the streets. When the doors were opened, the crowd surged in and soon filled every available inch of space. Thousands more crowded around the platform erected outside the hall. Inside and outside Revolutionary Russia was hailed while continual calls were made for Glasgow to follow the lead of Red Petrograd.

Tired and sweating, but keyed up to a terrific pitch of nervous excitement, I boarded the night train for London. I couldn't sleep. I couldn't even sit. I walked up and down the narrow corridor most of the journey. I reached London in the cold hours of the morning and started out to make contact. After considerable trouble, I got some of the boys together and had a talk with them about the strike. I wasn't favourably impressed. My impression was that they hadn't their hearts in the strike and would be not at all displeased if something happened to call it off. In Birmingham and Manchester this feeling became still more pronounced; only in Coventry and Sheffield was any spirit shown.

I returned to Glasgow on Wednesday and at night gave my report. I expressed the opinion that the strike would be over before we could get anything moving in the Clyde. Nevertheless it was necessary to do everything possible to get action in support of our English comrades as the Government, if it got away with the " comb-out " in England, would apply it ruthlessly to the Clyde.

This was generally agreed and the meeting, held in the large hall of the Central Halls in Bath Street, settled down to take stock of the position in the factories. The result was of the greatest importance to the future development of the movement. While most of the delegates reported a favourable situation in their factories or departments, every W.I.I.U. delegate present reported exactly on the same lines —such and such department, Parkhead or wherever it might be, meeting of the W.I.I.U. group was held, decided nothing could be done as workers were apathetic.

We drew attention to the fact that wherever a group of the W.I.I.U. still existed the movement was being held back. This marked a very big stage in the fight against this particular diversion.

During that week several of the strike leaders in London were arrested, then an agreement recommended by the officials was accepted and the strike called off. When the strike leaders came into court a week later, they were liberated with an admonition on promising to honour the agreement arrived at the previous Saturday.

CHAPTER VIII

DURING this period a campaign was being waged throughout the country for the holding of a National Convention in Leeds, to declare solidarity with the Russian Revolution and organize Workers' and Soldiers' Councils in Britain. The date fixed for the convention was June 3. Naturally the Clyde workers took a keen interest in the convention, and in the preparatory campaign. Maxton and several others were sent as delegates from the I.L.P. Tommy Bell and McManus headed a group from the S.L.P. I was there representing the Clyde Workers' Committee, whilst others represented a variety of peace organizations.

Trouble had been threatened and was expected in Leeds when the delegates arrived; but it didn't materialize. One or two slight incidents occurred but nothing worthy of note. About two thousand delegates packed the hall and were treated to a regular orgy of generalities on the beauty and holiness of bourgeois democracy. MacDonald, Snowden, Lansbury, and others went all out to sing the praises of parliamentary democracy. Russia had got her freedom at last; what they had all worked and prayed for. Soon Russia would have a " free parliament just like us." What a blessing to humanity this would be! It remained for Germany to follow Russia's lead and all would be well with the world. It developed into a regular debauch of sentiment.

In the afternoon, I managed to get the floor. I drew attention to the fact that the Revolution wasn't finished. Far from it. The workers and soldiers weren't making a revolution in order that nice bourgeois gentlemen could step in and take charge. They would hold on to power until they had defeated their own capitalists, but at the same time we had to take note that their heaviest battles would have to be fought against the capitalist class of Europe; that our job, if we were to assist the Russian workers, was to develop revolutionary action in this country, and so make it impossible for our capitalist class to interfere. I went on to propose particular activities that should be taken up immediately by the National Committee which the Convention was going to create.

In the *Herald* for June 9, column after column was given to MacDonald, Snowden and company. I got one inch of space. My speech was boiled down to the following:

" Mr. Gallacher (Glasgow) said: ' This conference seems to be agreed that the Russian revolution is definitely settled. But is it? No. The Russian workers and soldiers' delegates have the biggest fight on, not against the capitalists of Russia, but against the capitalists of other countries who are determined that they have to be beaten back. Give your own capitalist class in this country so much to do that it won't have time to attend to it.' "

The National Committee appointed was in line with the sentiments of the platform. If the Russian revolution wasn't finished, then it ought to be and they were going to do their damnedest to keep it from going any further. Of course, we didn't understand that at the time, and because of arrangements made for several district conferences, we continued to believe that something concrete would result. It took the November Revolution to free us from many illusions.

Thus passed June 3. On June 4 the deportation orders were withdrawn and Kirkwood, Clark, McManus and Messer were free to return to Glasgow. This gesture on the part of Lloyd George was made in the hope of banking down the feeling that was now rising higher than ever in Glasgow. Towards the end of 1916, he had given his famous interview to the American reporters, when he appealed for a clear field in order to give the Kaiser " a knock-out blow." How he let drive! But he missed the Kaiser and hit old man Asquith instead, knocking him clean out for the count.

Lloyd George now stood out as the champion death dispenser of Europe, and as such had been invited by the Glasgow Corporation to come north on June 29 to receive the Freedom of the City. Violent protests against this were coupled with the insistent demand that the Freedom of the City should be given to McLean, Kirkwood and the others.

Lloyd George was advised from all quarters that something would have to be done or there would be a revolt when he arrived; so the order was withdrawn and new hints were dropped about the early release of McLean. Thus we had the peculiar situation that as a consequence of his first visit, the deportation took place, and as a preparation for his second visit, the deportation orders were withdrawn.

On June 10, a new movement was launched in Glasgow; one that played an increasingly important part in the further development of the fight against the war. This was the Women's Peace Crusade, headed by Helen Crawfurd.

Helen, widow of a Free Church Minister, had taken an active part in the pre-war Suffrage Movement. She had experienced imprisonment and had hunger struck on several occasions and was quite impervious to police intimidation. She had a highly attractive personality and, no matter how hard the going, always maintained her composure and her charm. It was during the war that I met her first, and through all the hard struggles of that time, and the even more difficult days which followed, we remained the closest political associates and personal friends. She is now, owing to ill health, not so active in the movement, but in 1917 she was a mighty force in the great fight for Peace.

On Saturday, June 23, a reception was organized

in St. Mungo Hall to welcome back the deportees. This took the form of a social with short speeches from the deportees and from those who had been in prison.

" Big Davie " was there in his best form. With all his dramatic power he thundered: " Some workers you can find who are afraid of the Germans, but they forget one thing, they forget that the greatest Huns in Christendom are the capitalist class of Britain."

Davie was given a great reception, as was Maxton, who appeared for the first time in public as a " plater's helper."

The latter had been before the Tribunal and ordered to find work of national importance. One of the comrades, later Labour correspondent on a London newspaper, but then a plater, got Maxton fixed up with a job. He looked on the job as a joke, and we were all happy to know that Maxton was out of the hands of the military, as he was exceedingly popular with the shop stewards.

McManus spoke of the need for carrying the fight into the factories and for developing the political character of our work, and was followed by Messer, who appealed earnestly for a rebuilding of the organization. As all the best of the shop stewards were at this reception, Messer's appeal was of the greatest importance. The response it evoked showed how eager all were to get the movement back to its old strength.

Then came the great day, June 29, and the "Welsh Wizard" was in our midst once again. He had come to receive the "Freedom of the City." We had no general stoppage on the Clyde, but we succeeded in getting large numbers to cease work and to demonstrate from early morning. The greatest secrecy was maintained regarding the movements of the "great man" till the ceremonial drive took place. Rumours had been circulated (and were received with complete credence in certain circles) that we were going to kidnap him. Certainly every precaution was taken to protect him from such a fate. The suggestion was absurd, but we were certainly anxious to give him a "reception." Thousands of us were out for the purpose. But it was impossible to get anywhere near him. When he drove in an open carriage to St. Andrew's Hall, the spectacle was a sight for the gods. Ordinary police, mounted police, special police and military units lined up in front and behind, not only holding the "Welcoming" masses back, but also completely hiding the little fellow from view. He was receiving the "Freedom of the City" with the whole police force, supplemented by the military, detailed to protect him.

At the top window of a block of flats overlooking the west entrance to the hall used on this occasion, an old stalwart of the movement, Mrs. Reid, her white hair crowning a face alight with the flame of revolt against the mad slaughter of the war, was waving a great red flag.

From the distant place to which we had been forced back Kirkwood was shouting encouragement to her at the top of his stentorian voice, while the crowd gave her cheer after cheer. Before entering the hall, Mr. Lloyd George, always acutely conscious of the mood of the crowd, stood up in the carriage which had drawn to a stop, looked up at our comrade bravely waving the scarlet banner, raised his hat and gave her one of his most gracious bows. Then he looked over the heads of the military and police, towards the mass of workers, nodding his head as though to say, " You see, I'm a bit of a Red Flagger myself."

In this connection it may be well to remark that at the 1915 Christmas meeting he had already, in an effort to quell the din, informed us: " Boys, I'm as keen a Socialist as any of you, and when the war is over, I'll be back among you." This wily little gentleman has nothing to learn from his new friend Hitler. On the contrary there is evidence that Hitler and Goebels got a great deal of their demagogic stock in trade from David Lloyd George, the great master of that form of trickery.

The decision to confer the Freedom of the City on Lloyd George had aroused fury at all working-class meetings. This was directed towards the fight for the liberation of McLean and the return of the " deportees." The deportees were back in Glasgow, *so was McLean.* He had been brought to Duke Street for liberation, and the morning after the Freedom of the City had been granted to Lloyd George, the freedom of Glasgow was won for John McLean.

When the Lloyd George ceremony was over in St. Andrew's Hall, the central figure was hurried away to an hotel. We formed a procession through the streets, and made for Central Station Hotel, where we suspected he was. We were told he wasn't there, that he was leaving from Buchanan Street Station. We sent a contingent there to see if there was anything doing and to keep the station alive. All around the centre of the city, the workers were gathering and shouting for the release of McLean. Given a start there was no saying what might have happened. The workers were in a mood to tear up Glasgow by the roots. Police officials were running here and there, whispering and consulting. Then we were approached by police officials who informed us that the order for the release of McLean was already signed and that he would be out in the morning. Sure enough on Saturday morning, June 30, the prison gates were opened and McLean was with us once again, having served fourteen months of his three-year sentence.

What an effect that had on the movement; after the heavy blows we had had to endure, and from which we had staggered to our knees. Here was John McLean, furious fighter for the revolution, out once again in the leadership of the struggle, marching through the streets undaunted, irrepressible, holding high over his head the blood red banner of human brotherhood and human freedom. Glasgow's workers were risen to their feet again.

Two weeks later we organized a " welcome back " demonstration for McLean which far excelled anything of this character we had ever had before. Thousands of workers were unable to get into the hall. Although we had taken all available space, large hall and small hall, a great overflow reception had to be held outside. McLean was in real fighting form and roused his listeners to the highest pitch of enthusiasm with his exposure of the Allies' war aims and of the importance of the revolution going on in Russia. For McLean had no illusions about this. He saw the division of forces that was taking place and declared for a workers' Russia as the only possible " Free Russia." But our fight had to follow the same lines. All our forces had to be thrown into the struggle against the war, for the overthrow of the capitalist class, and for a workers' Britain. This argument may seem familiar and commonplace to many of my readers, but presented as it was then, in the midst of a world war, with all the fire and energy that was so much a part of McLean's very being, it had a tremendous effect. The next day the message of this great demonstration was carried into every factory and supplied the drive for meal-hour meetings and discussions all over the Clyde.

Just two days before this, on Sunday, July 8, there had been another historic scene in Glasgow. The Women's Peace Crusade came out in force.

Two great processions, one from the south side of the city, the other from the north, marched into the centre, George Square, where they joined forces for a march through the principal streets, to Glasgow Green. Helen Crawfurd and Agnes Dollan were in the leadership. They and the women associated with them did a great job. They showed the men how a demonstration should be organized. It was one huge blaze of colour. Banners of every description, well prepared streamers and slogans. It was a rich and attractive spectacle. Crowds of workers lined the route on the July Sunday as these thousands of women marched along. Not only lined the streets, but filled the streets marching along with them. " Down with the war." " Down with the warmakers "; from thousands of throats these slogans went roaring along the streets. At Glasgow Green, a resolution was put declaring friendship with the women of all countries and demanding an immediate peace without annexations or indemnities.

This march of the women and the demonstrations around McLean's release were of incalculable value in the preparations going on for a district convention of the workers' and soldiers' councils, fixed for Glasgow on Saturday, August 11. A similar district convention was held in London, but there the hall was invaded by a horde of half-mad " patriots " led by a gang of Australian soldiers and the meeting was completely broken up, and the platform party badly beaten up.

A wild campaign against the convention was

started in Scotland, especially in Glasgow, where it was branded as an insult to all Scottish " patriots." Letters were appearing from all and sundry, demanding action to stop it. Proposals were made that the soldiers should be organized to attack it, followed by the suggestion that instead of using the ordinary soldiers the wounded should be brought out of the hospitals to invade the convention; the idea being, of course, that we should be placed in a very awkward position if we resisted any attack that might be made on us by these victims of the war.

But we declared, and we meant it, that we would welcome the soldiers attending, whether they came from active service or from the hospitals, and those responsible for the agitation knew quite well how matters stood in that connection. They knew we had the solid support of the Discharged and Demobilized Soldiers' and Sailors' Federation and that we were strong enough to win over other soldiers who might be persuaded to attend. They soon dropped the " wounded soldier " proposal and centred attention on the magistrates. As a consequence they succeeded, a few days before the convention, in getting the magistrates to ban it.

This convention, like so many of our demonstrations, was to take place in the St. Mungo Hall. This hall was the property of the Scottish Co-operative Wholesale Society, and so was more easily available than any of the other large halls. But the magistrates' ban was too much for the Co-operative

Board to face, and at the last moment they cancelled the let.

We decided to change the convention into a demonstration and to hold it outside St. Mungo Hall at the same time we had fixed for the convention. This roused the opponents of the convention to a frenzy. They threatened to turn out all their forces and smash the demonstration. Ramsay Mac-Donald, who with Fairchild of the British Socialist Party had been allocated by the National Committee to the Scottish District as the principal speaker, came in for an exceptional share of abuse and insult. He was to be driven out of Glasgow in such a manner that he would never dare come back. With all this ferment going on we made our preparations. We organized a great muster of shop stewards to protect the demonstration in the event of an attack by our enemies. We lined them up four deep in the streets adjacent to the place of the demonstration, and then, when all the delegates and others participating were gathered around the platform, the shop stewards marched around and completely encircled the demonstration with an unbreakable barrier of resolute workers. When this manœuvre was completed, MacDonald was brought along in a taxi and led through an already prepared human channel to the platform. I was specially allocated to guard him, and a photograph of the platform, published in the Glasgow *Bulletin*, shows that I was taking my job seriously. He has quite a different kind of guard nowadays, although the bowler hat may lend them a measure of outward similarity.

It is interesting to recall an informal talk we had with MacDonald in connection with the preparations for this meeting. We were with him in the Glasgow office of the I.L.P., Messer, McManus, Tommy Clark and I, and a friend of mine from Paisley. In the course of our talk, Tommy Clark referred to instructions given to the shop stewards for dealing with any attempt to smash the meeting or to attack MacDonald. " What have you advised?' Ramsay asked, with an expectant smile. " Gie thim a dod on the bloody heid," Tommy answered. Was MacDonald pleased? You can bet he was.

We saw him safely on to the platform and the meeting got under weigh. Scouts were out keeping a wary watch for the " patriots," but except for a handful of rather timorous individuals who clustered together two or three streets away, nobody appeared and nothing whatever happened.

Shinwell, Chairman of the Glasgow Trades Council, opened the proceedings, and he let himself go. He went for the warmakers in real fighting style. " They're squirming now," he cried. " But before we've finished with them we'll make their teeth rattle." Yes, sir, " their teeth rattle." I must say I liked the sound of that and of many other similar expressions slung around by Shinwell. He was well to the Left at that time and extremely active. As a consequence, he was being singled out for special attention by the military authorities, his exemption as a trade union official being withdrawn. He was a brilliant speaker and one of the quickest-minded men I have known. This very sharpness of mind was the cause of much opposition which gathered around and against him. It made him often impatient and intolerant of the slower thinking comrades with whom he associated. But more serious than this was the dead set made against him by the Wheatley group in the leadership of the Labour Party in Glasgow. This sometimes took on a ferocious character, and the vilest attacks were made upon him. They succeeded to a great extent in isolating him from the general Labour Movement in Glasgow.

As MacDonald was relying on the Glasgow Labour Movement to secure his leadership of the party, he played up to all their prejudices, and so a few years after this meeting of the Workers' and Soldiers' Council, in 1922, in a private talk with the Scottish delegation at the I.L.P. Conference, he referred to Shinwell in his elegant way as "that cad Shinwell."

During all this period, Shinwell and I were very close friends, and on many questions our views were much the same. But now the breach between himself and his erstwhile enemies has been healed, and Shinwell takes a central position in the Labour movement. But his defeat of—"that cad "—MacDonald at Seaham in 1935 brought joy to the entire movement.

But to revert to this earlier period in Shinwell's career, when he spoke outside St. Mungo Hall at the

Workers' and Soldiers' demonstration, all his forensic ability was directed towards stirring up the hatred of the people against the capitalist class, and he made a good job of it. MacDonald, Fairchild of the B.S.P., Wheatley and several others spoke, but they all followed conventional lines of hailing the " new democracy " of " Free Russia " without taking note of the fact that the " new democracy " was going to assume a character different from anything in this or any other capitalist country. I had the responsibility of bringing this out and the response of the audience showed that they were well ahead of the vague generalizations put across by MacDonald.

Despite the weakness of policy in the main speeches, the demonstration was a huge success, the spirit rising to great heights at every reference to the fight against the war, for support of Revolutionary Russia and for the overthrow of the ruling class in this country. The complete failure of the " patriots " even to put in an appearance, after all their bombast in the Press, provided a still further encouragement for the pressing forward of the struggle.

During this period the Stockholm Conference was the subject of continual discussion in our various circles in Glasgow. We were all for the conference. Henderson, a member of the British Cabinet, was busying himself on this, and at one time it seemed practically certain to come off. But then the Allied leaders, who had hitherto appeared quite well disposed towards it, suddenly came out dead against

it, and the whole thing collapsed, leaving Mr.
Henderson standing on the " doormat."

As the days went by, it became quite clear who
were behind the move in the first place, and what
was the cause for their withdrawal later on. The
revolutionary elements in the different countries
wanted such a conference and were prepared to do
everything possible to bring it about. But the
" patriotic " socialists who were supporting their
respective governments, were not prepared to associate with anything of which their " masters " did
not approve. When the February Revolution took
place in Russia, the Allied Governments, especially
the British Government, endeavoured by every
means to use the revolution for the strengthening of
the Allied cause. All the Labour leaders in the
Allied countries took their cue, made the most
moving declarations welcoming the revolution, and
used the occasion to point out that if Germany
would follow Russia's lead and overthrow the
Kaiser and the militarists, democracy would triumph
all round and the war be brought to a satisfactory
conclusion. This was the big line of the Allied
" Social Patriots." The Germans must make the
next move. It was with a view to using the influence
of the Russian socialists in this direction, that
Henderson was allowed, and in fact encouraged, by
Lloyd George, to go ahead with the plans for
Stockholm.

For anyone who had any experience of Henderson, or of the other Labour leaders, during the war

knew one thing above all others—these men were prepared to do anything they were told, but not one of them was willing to do anything his immediate head had not sanctioned.

Henderson, therefore, with the approval of Lloyd George, went ahead with the organization of the Stockholm Conference, with the holy intention of using the Russian socialists as a battering ram against the German socialists. But as the campaign for the conference progressed, it became obvious from the discussions in the Petrograd Soviet that the central question was going to be the proposal for an immediate peace on the basis of no annexations and no indemnities.

A conference of this character in 1917, while it would have been of the greatest value for the international working-class movement, would have been a disaster for the warmakers of all countries, Allies as well as the Germans. So the heavy hand came down. Henderson was made the " goat." Lloyd George repudiated him and ordered him out of the Cabinet Room to stand on the " doormat " while he and the others decided his fate. One of his own colleagues, Geo. N. Barnes, was sent out as the Cabinet messenger boy to deliver the verdict. Henderson was sacked. Thrown out of the Cabinet. Very patiently he waited outside till the news was brought to him. The conveyor of the news, Geo. N. Barnes, got his job.

Everybody agreed that Henderson had got a dirty deal; that as a " lackey " to Lloyd George he had

willingly dropped and stamped in the mud every
shred of decency or principle he had ever possessed.
Yes, he got a dirty deal from his dirty master, whose
dirty work he had never hesitated to do. But the
dirty deal he got had no effect on his colleagues,
Barnes, Clynes and the others. There was no
question of their throwing up the job when their
" comrade " got victimized.

Far from that, they clung on tighter than ever
before. So much so, when the war ended and a
special one-day conference of the Labour Party in
London decided to finish with the Coalition, Clynes
refused to accept the decision and went to his union
to try to get its support in opposition to the
Labour Party. Only when his union turned him
down did he accept the decision and reluctantly
sever his connection with his Government position.

As for Barnes, he cynically finished with the
Labour Party, as did several others, and continued
to carry on as a " ticketed " dummy of Mr. Lloyd
George. Not only did the others carry on when
Henderson got the dirty kick, but at that time a
whole host of Labour Party and trade union leaders
were holding out their hands for tawdry decorations,
such as C.B.E., O.B.E., and the rest of them.

Brownlie, of the A.E.U., got " awarded " the
C.B.E. Shortly after the war he was one of the
speakers at a trade union meeting in the City Hall,
Glasgow. I got up to ask him a question. Kirkwood, who was sitting beside me, said, " Don't
forget the O.B.E." I didn't.

" Brother Chairman," I started, " I want to ask Brother Brownlie, O.B.E.——" (emphasis on the O.B.E.).

I didn't get any further; Brother Brownlie jumped to his feet.

" I want to correct Brother Gallacher," he said. There was considerable interruption, so he added, " It's all right, Brother Gallacher and I are good friends, but he has made a slight mistake. I'm not an O.B.E. I'm a C.B.E." Then with an oily smile, " Do you know what those letters stand for in my opinion—Common Bloody Engineer."

" No, Brother Chairman," I shouted, " they stand for Cowardly Bloody Engineer." Brownlie collapsed, and whatever atom of friendship ever existed between us, vanished never to return.

Not only was the Government handing out shoddy " honours " to all and sundry among the Labour Party and trade union leaders, but some bright spark conceived the wonderful idea of passing out medals to the factories. " The men in the factories are ' doing their bit ' as well as the men in the trenches. Let us honour them. And surely, if we ' honour ' them, they'll turn their backs on the wicked path they've been following and devote themselves to ' their King and Country.' "

When we heard of it on the Clyde, we could scarcely believe it was true. We thought it was someone's idea of a joke. But no. Medals were to be distributed to the " heroes " in the factories and the workers themselves had to select the " heroes."

A start was made in the torpedo factory outside Greenock, where Hughie Hinshelwood, a stalwart fighter for socialism, had carried on Marxian propaganda for many years. The torpedo factory got the first chance to select their " hero," and with one accord, absolutely, unquestionably unanimous their decision was recorded, the medal had to go to the lavatory attendant. What a roar of laughter shook the Clyde! Another " great idea " had gone all wrong. " Honours " were not tricking the workers on the Clyde.

In view of the fact that " honours " are once more being used for the purpose of war preparation, it is interesting to recall a statement which appeared in the *Herald* on September 1, 1917:

> " A fortnight ago we expressed the view that Labour had to choose between Stockholm and the ' Doormat,' since then our rulers have proceeded to make the choice ever clearer by placing no less than thirty-two Labour men in a new order of chivalry, *from which it is the highest honour for a Labour man to be excluded.*"

With continuous agitation going on all over the Clyde, it will be understood that there was a regular ferment in all the factories. Strikes were an almost everyday occurrence. But these were all in individual factories, or even departments of factories, striking on all kinds of issues, working conditions, price rates, bullying by the management and what not.

I had succeeded after much trouble, and through

the co-operation of the convenor of shop stewards at Beardmore's, Dalmuir, in getting a job there without the management being aware of it till after I was started. But no sooner was I there than a general trek began from all the neighbouring departments. All kinds of "old pals" wanted to have a talk with me. This attracted immediate attention, and within the shortest time, my presence was being discussed at the "head of the house." It wasn't considered politic to risk any new trouble by throwing me out, so after a few days, the manager of the department, Mr. Vickery, made a diplomatic approach with the offer of a "charge hand" job. But I had already, several years before, turned down a much better offer in the Albion, so I wasn't being taken in at Dalmuir. Dalmuir was one of our best centres and while I was there I was kept busy. Scarcely a week passed without a stoppage in one department or another, and whatever the stoppage I was brought in. We had a well-functioning factory committee that was capable of protecting the workers in every phase of workshop life.

The same applied to a number of other factories. It was now obvious that the time had come when a new advance in central organization was necessary. We therefore called a conference of shop stewards for September 15 to discuss the general formation of factory committees, and their central co-ordination. Almost four hundred shop stewards and factory delegates answered this call. I outlined the proposals we had to make. I showed that where a

strong factory committee existed, wages and working conditions were protected, bullying was completely stopped and 100 per cent trade unionism
was established. This latter point was of great
importance. Unscrupulous attempts of all kinds
had been made to present us as being opposed to
trade unionism. As a matter of fact no one could
be on any of our committees who was not in the
union. We were solid for the unions and because
of this fought against the destruction of the unions
threatened in the attempts of the "social patriots"
to hand them over to the warmakers. The same
danger faces the unions to-day. Sir Walter Citrine
(that's enough to make any decent trade unionist
vomit), and a few others are playing the same game
as the C.B.E.'s, and O.B.E.'s against whom our
fight had often to be directed.

After I had made my statement a representative
of the W.I.I.U. got up (they were not yet dead)
and proposed that we operate outside of, and in
opposition to the reformist unions. We killed that
at the start, and they got up and walked out.

This time, in contrast to the meeting in March,
instead of the meeting walking out and leaving
seven of us, the meeting remained and about seven
walked out. The Glasgow correspondent of the
Herald, reporting this conference in the issue of
September 29, said:

" The Clyde Workers' Committee had been definitely
established as the result of a workshop conference at the
week-end, with Willie Gallacher as chairman, and J. M.

Messer as secretary. Some delegates wanted to change the title, but the majority agreed to stick by the name which made the Committee famous all over Britain in the early months of 1916. Immediate steps are to be taken to link up the workers in every industrial establishment, and before long the Clyde Workers' Committee will be a greater power than ever. A small group of industrial unionists who wanted to work outside of the unions withdrew when their proposal was defeated."

While the movement in the factories was thus advancing, McLean was organizing a whole network of Marxist classes in the main industrial centres of Glasgow.

He had worked out a great series of studies and trained a splendid group of assistant tutors. With these in full operation the basis was laid and the plans prepared for the establishment of the Scottish Labour College. The work done by McLean during this winter of 1917-18 has never been equalled by anyone. His educational work would have been sufficient for half a dozen ordinary men, but on the top of this, he was carrying on a truly terrific propaganda and agitational campaign. Every minute of his time was devoted to the revolutionary struggle, every ounce of his extraordinary energy was thrown into the fight.

During September, an important strike took place which brought new forces into the anti-war struggle. For a considerable time, the Scottish Moulders had been demanding and negotiating for a 15s. increase in wages. They were offered 3s., and as a consequence, declared for strike action. Tommy Bell and Jock McBain, both of whom had hitherto clung to the abstractions of the S.L.P., broke their sectarian shackles and came out as the active leaders of this strike. They proved themselves during that period men who could be relied on in a crisis. Attacked from all sides they never lost their heads, but held the forces together in the most effective manner till the strike was concluded.

The Clyde Workers' Committee gave considerable support to the strike, and was ready, if the need arose and the request was made, to bring other workers into the struggle. Here, in a few terse sentences, Jock McBain, gives the cause of the strike and the success it achieved:

" The E.C. (of the Moulders) made a demand for a wage increase on December 1916, this the employers refused and E.C. sent the claim to Committee of Production, after some delay the claim was heard along with others, when we claimed we had special features about our claim that was only common to the Foundry, and such should have had special consideration; these were: We did not work piece work nor did we allow any overtime with the result we had no special means of augmenting our wages.

" An award of 3s. was made to various trades. This we at the time looked upon as an insult and started an agitation against such. We were informed that due to the Treasury Agreement we could not act.

" *We discussed the matter with the Moulders' delegate for Glasgow Branches attending the Clyde Workers' Committee,* and finally as the result of our agitation we built an emergency committee of representation from each branch in

Glasgow. Then extended the Committee throughout Scotland by throwing up an emergency committee in every town and linking them up through an emergency E.C. We took a ballot vote of members in Scotland on the question of the wage award and the ballot decided to down tools.

" We then called a strike for 15th September, 1917, in which all shops in Scotland participated. The dispute lasted for three weeks and a few days and terminated as the result of a joint deputation from Emergency Committee and E.C. of Union meeting the Minister of Labour in London. Previous to this Bell and I had visited London and interviewed Winston Churchill, who was then Minister of Munitions, and Churchill then gave the assurance that if we returned to work he would see consideration was given to our position.

" His promise resulted in the famous 12½ per cent which at first, was granted, but as the result of a general agitation the 12½ per cent became applicable to all employed in the Engineering Industry.'

This strike, like all other actions, was used to the utmost to arouse feeling against the war and the war-makers. The strength of this feeling may be gauged by the fact that at a meeting of the Scottish Advisory Council of the Labour Party on September 22, a resolution was passed by an overwhelming majority demanding an immediate peace, with no annexations and no indemnities. A. G. Walkden was present at this meeting representing the National Executive, but despite a whining message from Henderson which he read to the meeting, it took a further decision, demanding the withdrawal of the Labour Party from the Coalition. This was a bitter pill for

Henderson and the " Social Patriots " and a clear indication of the strength of the Anti-War Movement in Scotland.

In the meantime stirring news was coming through from Russia. The " Soviets " of workers and soldiers were assuming ever greater and greater importance. The Bolshevik slogan " All Power to the Soviets " was widely welcomed along the Clyde.

While Brailsford in the *Herald* was proclaiming the coming of disaster as a consequence of Bolshevik activity, the workers on the Clyde were already conscious of the fact that the Russian workers had to seize and hold on to power if the revolution was to be saved. Then came November and the Bolshevik revolution. While all the Labour leaders, including Lansbury, remained absolutely silent about this world-shaking event, the Clyde workers received the news with a wild shout of joy. For the first time in history, the workers, ordinary men and women, had thrown off their oppressors, had expropriated the parasites and taken the land and industries into their own hands.

A few of the De Leonite sectarians, looked with sour disfavour on the revolution. It couldn't be a " true " revolution as a social revolution could only follow fully developed capitalism. This was the strictly orthodox view of the sectarians. They couldn't see that in a period of crisis all the chances were in favour of the workers breaking through at capitalism's weakest link. In a discussion we had with some of these, one said, " Look at it (the revolution) through the S.L.P. telescope and you'll see that it cannot be a social revolution." To this I replied, " You fellows are looking through the telescope from the reverse end and it's impossible for you to see what's going on at the other end of it."

But the great bulk of the workers knew one thing, the one thing that mattered: the Russian workers had taken power, had overthrown the capitalist class and were now energetically preparing the way for an end to the war and for the reconstruction of Society. The call for an immediate peace with no annexations and no indemnities, the publication of the secret treaties, these were hailed with raptures of delight throughout the whole area. Huge meetings, night after night, rose to extraordinary heights of enthusiasm in support of the Bolshevik Revolution.

The *Herald*, writing of this period said: " Glasgow these days is wonderful. Yes, Glasgow is a tonic. If the Labour Party is weak, if Winstone* has not won, if the rest of civilization is on the road to decay, we still have got Glasgow. The movement in Glasgow ought to float itself as a limited liability company to supply backbone to the rest of the United Kingdom."

Nothing I could write, however, could give a clearer indication of the outstanding response of the Clyde workers to this great event than the following

* Labour candidate defeated just previously in a bye-election.

striking note written about the middle of December
1917:

" There is general discontent in Socialist and Labour
circles (in Glasgow) at what seems to be the apathy of the
official Socialist and Labour bodies in this country towards
our Bolshevik comrades. Their methods may not be
genteel, but they get there and their aim is our aim.
They are out to smash capitalism and imperialism, so
are we, and we should not stand still while they are being
attacked."

This was written by no less a person than P. J.
Dollan, the present City Treasurer in Glasgow.
Only the fact that the whole city was alive with
revolutionary fervour can explain the ultra-cautious
Pat, letting himself go in such a manner.

But even more significant of the effect of the
Bolshevik Revolution and the support it had
aroused amongst the workers was a resolution on
the Man-Power Bill, which was then being discussed, passed at a meeting of the trade union
officials on January 14, 1918. The resolution read:

" That we intimate to the parent bodies and the
Government that if the Government does not withdraw
the Man-Power Bill before the end of January, we will
advise our fellow workers on the Clyde to down tools,
and that we ask the Government to call an International
Conference to discuss peace terms at once."

While a small minority voted against the " down
tools " proposal, there was complete unanimity in
the demand for a Peace Conference.

This resolution set the parent bodies and the Government all a-twitter. Everything possible was done to damp down the agitation and to get an easy passage for the Man-Power Bill, but the opposition increased. The Man-Power Bill was designed to sweep the youth of the country into the maw of the Flanders death pit. From eighteen years upwards youth had to be driven to the slaughter. So we more correctly described this infamous Bill as the " Man-Slaughter Bill."

In a desperate attempt to allay the feeling against it Lloyd George decided to send one of his " war prodigies," Sir Auckland Geddes, to Glasgow to talk the trade unionists into a happier and more acceptable mood. The meeting was organized by arrangement with the trade union officials, who were to occupy the platform and take responsibility for the proceedings.

Before dealing with this meeting, which was one of the most remarkable of the whole series of war-time meetings, it would be well to revert for a moment to an important development in the work of the Women's Peace Crusade. This movement had been gathering strength by leaps and bounds. Kitchen meetings, street meetings, parades, leaflets and poster boards, all those and other activities were a continuous feature of their work. The effect on the general movement was incalculable. It is true to say that if you have the women with you there are no heights to which you cannot rise, and the women of Glasgow were coming into the fight in no uncertain manner.

As some of the Press said at the time: " The women are setting the heather on fire." In order to curb them, and to stem the general activity, an order was passed prohibiting the publication of printed matter, leaflets, etc., unless endorsed by the Press Bureau, a form of censorship then in operation.

To Helen Crawfurd and her colleagues this was simply a stimulus to still greater activity. A spate of leaflets was published in defiance of the order. Then on December 13, a march on the City Council was organized to demand the withdrawal of the order and to get a declaration in favour of an immediate peace. The police turned out in force to protect the council and to keep the women out, but under the leadership of Helen Crawfurd and Agnes Dollan, the women stormed the building and forced their way right into the Council Chamber.

All around George Square, in the faces of the police, women were openly distributing " illegal " leaflets in defiance of the order. Wild scenes occurred as the police tried to put the women out of the building, wilder scenes still when it was found that a number had been arrested. In the evening when the factories were emptied of their thousands of toilers and news of the day's doings was spread around, the greatest excitement prevailed. It was touch and go that night for a real outbreak of trouble. Mass meetings were held in every part of the city. Angry murmurs grew into a roar of rage. But the authorities discreetly kept the police out of the way and so the night passed without untoward incident.

It was in an atmosphere of this kind that Sir Auckland Geddes dropped to tell the shop stewards the merits of the "Man-Slaughter Bill." The meeting was called for the City Hall on January 28, 1918. The night before the meeting we had a conference of the leaders of the Clyde Workers' Committee. It was decided that I should obtain charge of the meeting and make arrangements for a resolution against the bill and in favour of an immediate armistice. This resolution was to be moved by Arthur McManus and seconded by James Maxton.

On Monday evening, half an hour before starting time, the City Hall was packed with about 2,500 shop stewards and factory representatives. Slogans against the war were shouted from every part of the Hall. Then songs, some of them very rough but very much to the point. One of these, "To Hell with Lloyd George" and a variety of other people including the Kaiser and his cousin, was sung by Maxton in I.L.P. circles for many years after. But the favourite one was to the tune of "Pull for the shore, Sailor." The chorus went:

" Go to the war, workers, go to the war,
   Heed not the Socialists, but wallow in gore;
   Shoulder your rifle, worker, don't ask what it's for
   Let your wife and children starve and go to the war."

While the singing and shouting was going on McGill of the Herald League Bookshop could be seen passing round the hall selling his papers, prominent amongst which was a special number of the *Socialist*. The front page was a picture of a barbed wire entanglement and tattered torn bodies in all kinds of ghastly shapes. This picture was bordered along the top and down the sides with great red blobs like drops of blood. It was headed by the notorious phrase, " A Bundle of Bloody Rags."

The platform party came on right to the minute —several trade union officials, with Sir Auckland Geddes and a couple of unknown companions. As they mounted the platform the audience rose and sang the " Red Flag." The platform party had to stand at attention till it was finished. When they were seated McGill stepped forward and said to Geddes, " Here, do you want the *Socialist* ? " " Yes," said Geddes, and he and the others bought their copies.

Willie Lawson of the Joiners was in the chair. As soon as he rose the storm broke. It was impossible to hear a word. After a whispered consultation with Geddes, the latter got up, but this only made things worse. Will Fyffe then walked up to the front of the platform and said to Lawson, " Willie Gallacher's here. If you invite him up, things will quieten down."

" We don't want Willie Gallacher," said Lawson, " we know what that means."

"All right," said Fyffe, "I just thought I'd mention it."

Two or three of the other trade union officials tried to speak, without avail. Then, after another whispered consultation with Geddes, Lawson beckoned to Will Fyffe to come over. "Ask Willie to come up," he said.

In the midst of a terrific din I stepped on to the platform. Immediately the noise changed into a roar of greetings. After a minute or two I got silence and then proposed that we give Geddes half an hour to state his case, after which we would have questions, and then Arthur McManus would move a resolution. This was agreed to, so Geddes took the floor.* He got a very quiet hearing throughout, the only interruptions being on two occasions when he tried to work in a bit of cheap demagogy. The first was when he thought he was sailing along all right, and said, "You know, boys, when I came on to the platform and heard you singing the ' Red Flag,' my heart was with you." I had quite a job getting them to keep their seats. The second was when he tried the human touch. " I want to see the war finished," he declared, "when I think of my

---

* When Clynes came to Glasgow a little later on he had Shinwell for chairman, supported by a group of trade union officials and Labour Councillors. Pandemonium started as soon as he appeared on the platform. I came into the hall late and was nearly deafened with the clamour. Shinwell got his eye on me and sent Councillor George Kerr down into the hall to ask me to come up and restore order. I refused. I had the opinion that Clynes was not the least contemptible of all the Social Patriots and I was not prepared to associate with him in any way.

wife standing out on the queue." He didn't get any further. " Christ," I said, " can't you get on with the 'Man-Slaughter Bill' without that damned nonsense? You're making things impossible."

He got on with his speech but said nothing about the Bill. I never heard a man flounder about so much as he did that night. I never knew a man so glad when his time was up.

Then came questions, and there were plenty of them. He could do nothing with them. A young comrade named Brennan put a couple about the secret treaties. Geddes got up—but evaded them.

He sat down and asked me, " Is it true, Gallacher, about these secret treaties? "

" Of course," I replied. " E. D. Morel has written a pamphlet about them."

" I never heard of them before," he confessed.

When he got up to answer the next question I gave the sign to a little fellow named McGlynn whom I had posted in the balcony convenient to the platform. McGlynn was eighteen years of age and undersized, about five feet in height. He was an apprentice in Dalmuir and had come over to me that day with his calling-up papers. He said to me: " Dobson (the foreman) says I'll have to go." I said to him, " You come up to the City Hall to-night and I'll fix things for you."

At my signal he came on to the platform. " Stand beside Mr. Auckland," I said. He stood at his side, and what a contrast! Geddes, about 5 feet 10 inches and well built, and the little undersized eighteen-year-old!

"Now, sir," I said to Geddes, "will you tell this meeting of shop stewards that you're going to send this little fellow out to save you from the Germans?"

Geddes looked at McGlynn. "What age are you?" he asked.

"Eighteen," replied McGlynn.

"No," shouted Geddes, "we won't send him out. Nobody under nineteen."

"Good enough," I said, when the roar of laughter had subsided, "I got his papers to-day and destroyed them. Was I right?"

"Quite right," he said. McGlynn went off quite happy.

The baiting of the unhappy Minister having gone far enough I called on Arthur McManus. "Little Arthur" was a brilliant speaker and one of our best agitators. When he got up on a seat to move the resolution he got a great demonstration. While the demonstration was going on Geddes was saying to me, "You know, Gallacher, this is the most amazing experience I've ever had. I never could have believed it." I said, "Wait till you see the vote for this resolution and you'll get a real eye-opener."

When the demonstration died down McManus put the resolution. Then in a brilliant speech he riddled the case for the continuance of the war, ending up with "Not another man for the criminal war for trade and territory! An immediate end to it. This is our challenge to the Government. For this we are fighting and will go on fighting! " Then, just as the cheering stopped, it started again when Jimmy Maxton was called on to second the resolution.*

Geddes was certainly impressed. After Maxton had seconded, I said a few words from the platform, then called for a show of hands—all in favour to put up both hands.

The great packed hall, above and below, was a sea of hands. " There," I said to Geddes, " is the answer of the Clyde to your Man-Power Bill." " Amazing, amazing," was all he could say. The " Red Flag " once again, after which out on to the streets, form up four deep and a march through the city for a midnight meeting at George's Square. What a night it was!

Next day the Press was out full cry. The Great German offensive was on. Britain was fighting with her back to the wall and a gang of traitors was doing all it could to help the Germans.

On the heels of Geddes came another visitor. An old friend from the days of the Dilution Commission, Sir Lyndon Macassie, now in charge of the Shipyard Labour Commission. How these fellows

* (1) That having heard the case for the Government as stated by Sir Auckland Geddes this meeting pledges itself to oppose the Government to the very uttermost in its power call for men.

(2) That we insist on and we bind ourselves to take action to enforce the declaration of an immediate armistice on all fronts.

(3) And that the expressed opinion of the workers of Glasgow from now on is that our attitude should be to do nothing at all in support of carrying on the war but to do everything we can to bring the war to a conclusion.

kept themselves afloat on the tumultuous sea of war was a wonder to all mankind. Eliza never jumped the ice-floes with anything like the agility with which they jumped from one Commission to another.

This time Macassie had a whole string of regulations for tying up the workers in the yard. He addressed a general meeting of trade union officials and put his proposals before them. We opposed them and showed that they were all directed against the freedom of the workers with not a regulation of any kind to control or check the profits of the employers.

He went back to London without having achieved any success, but nevertheless determined to get his regulations forced through.

At the subsequent meeting of the Allied Trades Committee, we discussed the new proposals and registered our unyielding opposition to them. I drew attention to the fact that in such situations we were always in the weak position of being on the defensive. The Government representatives presented proposals, we opposed them, but they simply kept going at it, till they got them through. Why not draw up our own document as a counter to the Government, and then with the support of our members fight the Government?

While one or two of them were reluctant to commit themselves to any definite proposals the general opinion was for this course. Especially strong support came from John McKenzie of the General

Labourers' Union and from the new chairman of the committee, Willie Lawson of the Joiners. (Sharp, our old chairman was now with the employers.) McKenzie was an outstanding man on the committee. A few years previously a highland labourer in Ballachulish, he had shown much enterprise and vitality and had now become the Scottish organizer of the union. Despite the fact that he was one of the oldest trade union officials in Glasgow, his position on the committee was anything but happy. He was a labourer representing labourers, and craft prejudices were still very much alive amongst the others. This brought him into close association with me. He was like a Jew on a committee of half-concealed anti-Semites, with the revolutionary as his natural ally.

Willie Lawson was quietly dressed, quiet mannered, and quiet spoken. He looked for all the world like a fairly comfortable little shopkeeper and the last man anyone would associate with " Red " activities. He is now a Justice of the Peace in Govan, but on this particular issue, Willie did his " bit " and did it well.

He, McKenzie and I were appointed as a small committee to draw up a document. In consultation with McManus and Messer, I made a draft. This was worked on by McKenzie and Willie Lawson, and after completion presented to, and accepted by the committee as a whole. It was then sent to the responsible Ministers, as the only terms on which we were prepared to come to an agreement with the Shipyard Labour Commission.

A day or two later we were invited to send a deputation to London to discuss the question there. Another two members were added to the already appointed small committee and the five of us set off for London. We got first-class railway tickets and expenses. £10 each, return, it cost, besides other expenses and our interview when we got to London lasted for half an hour and achieved nothing.

We went into a hotel in the Strand. Sir Lyndon made a short statement on the Government's proposals. Willie Lawson told him quickly but firmly that we were not there to discuss his proposals, we were there to discuss our proposals and nothing else. Sir Lyndon made two or three efforts to get around that, but in vain. Willie stuck to his guns and we stuck by Willie. Macassie saw it was no use, so he abruptly ended the proceedings and we had successfully jammed the Shipyard Labour Commission.

Havelock Wilson, the seamen's secretary, and greatest patriot of all the trade union leaders, fresh from his victory in getting the sailors to refuse to sail the ship in which MacDonald was booked to travel to the Stockholm conference, came to Glasgow about this time for a great jingo meeting.

Tickets were printed and considerable care was taken in their distribution, but early on we came into possession of some and these were used for making others. We had a thousand or so printed and distributed with advice to our chaps to be along early. But Wilson wasn't depending on tickets alone to secure a meeting. He brought a crowd of gangsters from the North of England to St. Andrew's Hall and served them out with a considerable supply of booze. It was one of the earliest applications of fascist methods in this country, with guaranteed police protection.

Lord Provost ("Half-a-Spud") Dunlop, took the chair, accompanied by a number of Glasgow celebrities, all of them prepared to sacrifice their last relative in the cause of a righteous war.

The chairman got a boisterous and undignified reception. A short time before the civic authorities in Glasgow had run a great propaganda campaign on the need for conserving food. A poster was issued and stuck up throughout the city, which read:

" The Wolf is at the Door "
" Eat Less Bread."

to which we attached the following question and answer:

" But why eat less bread? "
" Oh, leave a little for the wolf."

This poster was bad enough, but then they had a brain wave. Get important people to tell the world, and especially the workers, how little *they* were eating. And who should take the lead but the first citizen, the Lord Provost. Judge of the feelings and the expression of these feelings that took place when we found tramcars and walls decorated with a poster giving us the daily starvation diet of this worthy old gentleman.

Outstanding in his " genuine " daily diet was the leading item in the principal meal of the day, " half a potato." Yes, sir! There it was plain for all to see—" half a spud."

I believe I heard more obscene remarks about that than I had ever heard in my life before. So " Half-a-Spud " opened the meeting and it opened, if not with a flourish of trumpets, with something that had a strong family resemblance to it. As quickly as possible the chairman got back to his seat and let Havelock Wilson take his place.

When Wilson rose a minor riot broke out in the hall. We had a strong organised group in the centre and were easily able to hold off the half-drunk gangsters, but wherever they were able to get anyone isolated they were utterly savage. George Buchanan, now M.P. for Gorbals, was one who got a very rough handling. Another was Rosie, then twelve or fourteen years of age, now the wife of Peter Kerrigan, a leader of the Communist Party in Glasgow.

She with a little companion was in the balcony cheering on those down below. With her companion she was dragged to the door and violently thrown into the corridor. But in the centre of the hall the so-called " stewards " were knocked down like ninepins. For almost an hour Wilson stood on the platform without the chance of uttering a word. The roaring and the fighting was continuous.

Outside there were several hundred policemen but they could not be brought in.

To have brought them in would have meant bringing in an avalanche. For there were thousands of workers who could hear the battle raging inside, and all the power the police could muster, was directed towards keeping these outside. If the police had made a move towards the hall there would have been a rush that nothing could have checked. After an hour's silent posturing on the platform, Wilson sat down, the organ blared forth " Rule, Britannia " and " God Save the King," and "Half-a-Spud" led his sorry assembly of " fighters from the rear " off the platform.

This was the protest of the Glasgow workers against the attempt to prevent the British delegation attending the Stockholm conference.

A few days later I got a message asking me to visit the office of a well-known legal man, after business hours, as he had something important he wanted to see me about. I went to see him. He informed me that he was in close touch with certain leaders of the Liberal Party and that he had been asked to inform us of the fact that the Cabinet was discussing the advisability of arresting us on a charge of " High Treason." He was to advise us to walk very warily. According to his information Carson was vehemently urging this course but the more cautious members were afraid it would have a bad effect abroad and that such procedure would knock a bad dent in the holy Ark of Righteousness, which represented Britain's reason for participation in the war. One bright fellow suggested that our " immunity " should be withdrawn and the military left to pick us up for the army. I had a laugh at that one. I said, " They might arrest us for high treason, they might even put us in the Tower, but one thing they'll never be mad enough to do and that is put us in the army. That's the last place on earth they'll dream of putting us."

I reported this conversation to the boys but it didn't worry them overmuch. We had something else to worry about. Sometime before I had been booked to address several meetings in Belfast, on February 9 and 10, Saturday and Sunday. Already Belfast " Patriots " were objecting to my visit and trying to incite the workers against me. Following the Geddes meeting and the publication of our resolution the storm rose to a terrific height. " Loyal Ulster Protestants," according to the Press, would never tolerate the presence of a traitor.

The two or three boys who were organizing the meetings were getting a bit jumpy and suggested postponing them to a more favourable opportunity. But the committee was of the opinion that this would be fatal. Once postponed they'd never be held and the prestige of the committee would suffer seriously as a consequence. So on the Friday night I set out for Belfast. I had to take the short sea route from Stranraer to Larne as the submarines were threatening the Irish Coast. With all lights out and with a strange tenseness pervading the ship, it was anything but a pleasure sail, but I must confess that I wasn't thinking so much of " submarines " as I was of " loyal Protestants." I had worked in Belfast before the war and I knew how far they could go, if they once got started. My only hope was that they wouldn't get started.

The first public meeting was on Saturday night in the Engineers' Institute. We had had a small meeting of supporters in the afternoon. The hall, which wasn't very big, was packed immediately the doors opened. Prompt on starting time the chairman and I stepped on the platform. The chairman was a quiet, inexperienced comrade and a Catholic. He was very nervous, for it was easy to feel the tension in the hall.

He stepped forward to the table to open the meeting when a big fellow at the back stood up and shouted, " Before this meeting opens I want to ask Mr. Gallacher, is he loyal to his King? " The chairman was speechless. I said to him, " Sit down and I'll handle this." To the other I replied, " That's a stupid question. You know I am a revolutionary and that the only loyalty I have is to the working class."

That started it. One after another they got up and bawled questions and made assertions, but it was always one or other of a group at the back; the main body of the audience were obviously undecided. This group tried every dirty trick to get something started. I kept lashing out at them but always in such a way as to keep the rest neutral.

It went on for twenty minutes and I had them beat. The leader shouted: "You're a traitor to your country. We won't wait in the hall and listen to you." "All right," I replied. "Good night; we'll do our best to get on without you."

The audience had been more and more expressing their support of the platform but this set them off laughing and the gang at the back was finished. Behind their leader about a dozen or so walked out and I then went ahead and had a splendid meeting.

On the Sunday afternoon when we went round to the same hall for a meeting at three o'clock, we found the street outside crowded with people waiting to get in, but the hall door was closed. Pressure had been brought to bear on the official committee and the lease of the hall was cancelled without any notice.

The Belfast Branch of the I.L.P. put their hall at our disposal for the afternoon and night meetings. At both meetings the hall was packed, a side-room off the hall and the stairway leading up to the hall doors were also packed and not a murmur of opposition anywhere. The "loyal Protestants" in the factories of Belfast were seeing the war as the "disloyal Bolsheviks" of Glasgow were seeing it. When the big fight came at the end of the war, Belfast was in it to a man.

While all this was going on we had no publicity except the distortions and slanders of the yellow Press. None of the Socialist papers would touch us. They knew that immediately they published any-

thing of a serious character they would be closed.
This is as far as the *Herald* was prepared to go,
when, on March 2, it printed the following:

"WILLIE GALLACHER'S TOURS

" Willie Gallacher, Chairman of the Clyde Workers'
Committee, was in Sheffield at the week-end and had a
fine reception from a crowded propaganda meeting on
Sunday evening. In the afternoon he spoke at a conference of shop stewards and informed them as to the
situation on the Clyde.

" A couple of weeks ago he had four successful meetings at Belfast, although the capitalist Press tried to
create the impression that the Glasgow 'Bolshevik' met
with hostility."

But not a word about the Geddes meeting. It
was the same with the others. We had discussed
bringing out another paper to replace the suppressed *Worker* but we couldn't get a printer. The
I.L.P. did not refuse to print it, but told us we
ought not to ask, as the raid in 1916 had just about
cost them their press and another such raid would be
the end for them. We had no plant of our own that
we could use and so suffered one of the worst of all
disadvantages, the lack of a paper. This is one of the
problems that will always arise in such situations.
One that must be seriously prepared for.

Even as we were fighting the Man-Power Bill,
and Shipyard Labour Commission, other things
were happening. Two outstanding events, in the
midst of a continuous stream of movement.

John McLean, indomitable revolutionary fighter, had been appointed Soviet Consul for Scotland. The proletarian revolution had honoured one who was well worthy of the trust placed in his hand. To his multitude of tasks were added new ones. The Bolshevik Government wasn't recognized and many Russian families found themselves in difficult circumstances. With the assistance of a Russian comrade named Shamus, who acted as his secretary, he threw himself into his new task with his accustomed energy and the many hard-hit Russians found him a ready friend and adviser.

A monster demonstration, with a march through the streets to the Glasgow Green, followed his appointment, with resolutions approving of the choice and pledging solidarity with the Soviet Government.

Then about the same time the decision was taken by the May Day Committee to hold the May Day demonstrations on May 1, instead of the first Sunday. May 1 fell on a Wednesday which meant closing down the factories in the middle of the week. This was the last straw so far as the Press was concerned. Hitherto they had sneered at the very idea of May Day. Now they begged us to have it on Sunday and everybody would welcome it. When this failed to make any impression, then came the demand for its suppression.

From the beginning they recognized the futility of appealing to the workers to remain at work. They knew the workers were going to respond to the call, so did the authorities; therefore to ban it would have made no difference so far as the stoppage went. 250 organizations or branches of organizations had signified their intention of participating, including the Co-operative Wholesale Society which had decided to give all the employees the day off with pay.

The Clyde Workers' Committee sent out a call to all shop stewards to see that everything was done, not only to stop the factories, but to get the maximum number of workers in the streets.

When May 1 arrived we had a demonstration that surpassed anything ever seen before. George Square, where the procession assembled, and the streets adjoining it were packed with the gathering crowds. Column after column went marching through the Square—bands playing, flags flying, never-ending shouts against the war. When passing near certain newspaper offices, there was angry talk about paying them a visit, and with very little encouragement an attack would have been launched against them. The " power of the Press " may be great, but the power of an aroused and angry working class is a thousand times greater. It might be well for the gentlemen of the Press to take note of that.

In the midst of that great day of proclamation of international solidarity, was heard a slogan which had been heard often in Glasgow during 1916 and the beginning of 1917—" Release John McLean." Yes, he had been arrested again.

In the beginning of April Shamus, his secretary,

was arrested and deported to Russia; then on April 15, McLean was arrested. He was charged with sedition in that he did incite the lieges to rob food stores, attack the lawful authorities and a whole host of other misdeeds.

The Glasgow *Herald* on April 16, commenting on the arrest said: " The indictment brought against McLean gives extracts from ten speeches said to have been delivered by him in Glasgow, Lanarkshire and Fifeshire. It is alleged that in these addresses he advocated a revolution—that the workers should raise the Red Flag in the same way as their brothers in Russia had done, and should copy the method of the Russian revolution and strike their first blow for the revolution on May 1. That he urged the breaking through of laws and advised that unless the Government followed the example of the Russian revolutionaries workmen should down tools.

" Accused is alleged to have said further that the workers should seize the Lord Provost of Glasgow and the others as hostages for the safety of the Revolutionary Committee. That they should seize also the Glasgow City Chambers, Post Office, banks, the offices of the Glasgow *Herald* and *Daily Record*, and the food stores and ships on the Clyde. That they should destroy the police offices or seize them and put the police inside them. That they should seize the coal mines and should go to the farmers and get food and burn the farmhouses if they did not get food." That gives some idea of the length to which the authorities were prepared to go in manufacturing a case against a revolutionary fighter like McLean.

He was committed for trial in the High Court and refused bail. From the Glasgow Green on May Day we marched to Duke Street Prison where he was confined and made a demonstration at the prison gates. Special forces were organized on the prison side of the gates lest we should attempt to force an entrance.

CHAPTER IX

ON May 9 John McLean came up for trial. Again he defended himself against a crowd of police and special police witnesses who " testified," in the most obviously well-prepared way, their various stories about McLean's meetings. Surely there can be no greater scandal than what is called " police evidence." In the officers came, one after another, with parrot-like repetitions of carefully coached and memorised " stories."

On the most appalling testimony a jury of little " patriots," led by a " patriot " judge, found McLean guilty and the " patriot " judge sentenced him to *five years' penal servitude*. This savage sentence aroused the whole country and a widespread campaign was started immediately for McLean's release.

The Government, having blundered, tried to soften down the harshness of the sentence by allowing McLean privileges that are only allowed normally to first division prisoners. This weakness, expressed in the hesitancy to carry out the terms of their own sentence, only served to strengthen our determination to get complete liberation.

One thing we had decided and had openly

declared. George N. Barnes, the sitting member for the Gorbals Division of Glasgow, would not be allowed to speak in Glasgow while McLean was in prison. Barnes was a member of the Government, one of Lloyd George's " yes-men," and as such had been discarded by the Gorbals Labour Party, which had chosen McLean to replace him.

Barnes came to Glasgow for a series of meetings in August, but before he came we had a visitor of an entirely opposite type. A man who had won great honour by selfless devotion to a cause for which he was prepared if need be to sacrifice life itself. With all kinds of " labour " men falling over themselves to lick the boots of their " masters," a man like E. D. Morel shone out like a beacon.

On Sunday, June 23, he came, accompanied by Ramsay MacDonald, to speak in the Metropole Theatre, Glasgow. The meeting was timed to start at seven o'clock, doors open at six-thirty. Yet while it was impossible for a " patriot," no matter who or what he was, to hold an open public meeting in Glasgow, already at three o'clock in the afternoon a queue started forming to give a real Glasgow welcome to Morel. By opening time there were sufficient gathered around the theatre to have filled it half a dozen times over. The theatre was packed out and a huge overflow meeting was held in an open space across the way. I was asked to take charge of the overflow, which I did, assisted by MacDonald and several others. Morel, whose heart was not too strong, confined himself to the inside meeting. But what a reception he got. Outside, across the way, we could hear cheering as though they wanted to lift the roof off.

It was at this meeting that MacDonald declared that coming to Glasgow was like getting " a spiritual bath," it " cleansed the soul." It would take all the " spirit " of the Royal Dutch or Shell Mex to clean whatever remains of his soul now.

But on that fine Sunday we weren't thinking far enough ahead to see what would become of MacDonald. We admired Morel and we turned out in full strength to do him honour.

As I have already said it was impossible for the " jingoes " to hold an open public meeting in Glasgow. Whenever these meetings were tried they were invariably turned into demonstrations against the war. But one meeting for which extraordinary precautions were taken and which we failed to penetrate with any force, was a meeting addressed by Winston Churchill. The conservative and other patriotic clubs were utilized to secure a hand-picked audience. No matter how we canvassed we couldn't get our hands on a ticket. From one ticket we could have reproduced as many more as we wanted. This we had done with great success at a previous meeting, but now they were on their guard.

Only within an hour or two of the meeting taking place did I, through the courtesy of a Conservative friend, become the possessor of one. It was too late to get in touch with the others or to get anything done. All I could do was to present

myself at St. Andrew's Hall where the meeting
was being held, on the chance of picking up some
others who had been similarly successful. I was
dressed up with bowler hat on head and an umbrella
on my arm and looked the petty-bourgeois " patriot " to the life. I had no difficulty in passing the
observant " scrutineers " at the doors and made my
way to a seat in the centre of the hall. I looked
around but saw no sign of a friendly face. I saw
plenty of special police, however. They decorated
all parts of the hall. The organ was going full blast,
blaring forth popular " patriotic " music while the
audience sat straight-backed and solemn.

The platform party came on to an extra blare
from the organ, then after a few preliminaries from
the chairman, Churchill got up to do his stuff. He
knew the sort of audience he had and he played up
to it. A tricky master of language, he had obviously
taken special pains for this occasion. If ever there
was a holy war, this was one. Not a man there had
wanted war, but once forced into it not a man
would falter. I watched my chance and when he
stopped for dramatic effect, I got up on the seat and
started what would have been a great speech.
I said, " Mr. Chairman, if the soldiers had the same
privilege as Churchill, the privilege of packing up
and coming home, the war would soon end,
but——" I got no further. For a few seconds the
suddenness of my intervention shocked the audience
into silence. Churchill was standing with his mouth
half-open in a condition of momentary paralysis.

Then there was a roar and a rush of the special police. Half a dozen of them grabbed me and wrestled me over to the side of the hall. I was jammed against the wall and almost suffocated when I heard a shout from the front of the hall, " Stick it out, Willie, I'm coming! " It was Phil McEwen, secretary of the Discharged Soldiers' Federation. He was followed by Neil McLean (now M.P. for Govan). That made three of us and for quite a time we gave a good account of ourselves. But Churchill having got his faculties working again made the most of his chance. He played up with an occasional brilliant aside to the great delight of the audience. He had them roaring with laughter at our expense. I am prepared to testify before God and man that Churchill, brilliant orator and erratic politician, can " hand it out."

My next experience of him was in the General Election of 1922 when we were both contesting Dundee, a double-barrelled constituency. He was one of the sitting members but he and his colleague suffered a heavy defeat at the hands of " Neddy " Scrymegeour (a freak "Prohibition" candidate) and E. D. Morel, who won a seat for Labour. I was the Communist candidate and finished at the bottom of five nominees.

On the night of the declaration of the poll we were all gathered at a first floor window of the Caird Hall from where the returning officer read out the results to the crowd below. There were enthusiastic shouts for Scrymegeour and Morel, interspersed with occasional noisy jeers for Churchill. After Neddy Scrymegeour had thanked God for his great mercy and Morel had thanked his supporters, the returning officer asked Churchill if he would like to say something. Churchill was standing with his back to the window wrapped in deepest gloom. He nervously plucked at his bottom lip, with his eyes focused far away on happier times and happier places while his good lady sat at his side softly sobbing in sympathy with her lord and master.

The returning officer coughed and repeated his question. Slowly the head of the great one moved in automatic negative.

The returning officer was going to close the proceedings, but I stepped forward and said "I am going to speak." It was as though an electric current had gone through Churchill. He drew himself up, his eyes focused on his surroundings, his body half turned though his feet never moved. Just for the moment my example almost nerved him to the effort but he was lacking in the essential stuff, lacking in " intestinal co-ordination " as he himself would probably put it. His body fell back into line with his feet. His chance was gone. Mr. Churchill can " dish it out," of that there is not the slightest doubt, but Mr. Churchill cannot " take it."

In the beginning of August Barnes came to the city. The campaign for the release of McLean was in the forefront of our activities, and at his first meeting held in the Electreum Cinema the secretary of the Discharged Soldiers' and Sailors' Federation and I informed Barnes that neither he nor any other member of the Government would be allowed to speak till McLean was released. The workers saw to it that this pledge was carried out.

Here is the wretched comment of the *Herald* for August 24:

" George Barnes has experienced a very rough weekend in the city of Glasgow. Discharged soldiers, trade unionists, socialists and others have all united together to make it quite impossible for him to address his constituents in a peaceable manner. We regret very much indeed that he was not allowed to enjoy perfect freedom of speech."

John McLean " enjoying " the confinement of Peterhead prison, thousands of young boys " enjoying " the unspeakable agony of barbed wire entanglements and the lung-tearing death of poison gas, but " we regret very much indeed that he was not allowed to enjoy perfect freedom of speech! "

Barnes's attempt to address his constituents was connected with the preparations that were going on for an election in the winter. As has already been said, the Labour Movement in his constituency refused to have anything to do with him. The only nomination before it was that of John McLean who had been nominated by the B.S.P. The local party was prepared to accept McLean but the war-time executive wanted the local men to support Barnes, which they flatly refused to do.

In the Glasgow constituencies the I.L.P. was well to the fore with candidates, and the greatest activity was now being turned towards constituency organisation.

As these preparations went on for what was an exceptionally important phase of the struggle, the political weakness of the leadership of the Clyde Workers' Committee manifested itself, although unfortunately we were unable to see it.

McManus, independently of the rest of us, accepted the nomination of the S.L.P. for an absolutely hopeless fight in Halifax, the seat held by the then Speaker. We didn't consider this our business any more than he did. But while he was prepared to go into a constituency for a " propaganda " election campaign, the rest of us were not prepared to consider constituencies at all. We had a " supreme contempt " for the parliamentarians, having at that time no understanding of the importance of revolutionary parliamentarism as a means of combating reformism and stimulating the workers in the struggle for the overthrow of capitalism.

We left the field clear for the reformists. In the factories we were stronger than ever and were busily engaged in preparing a campaign for a shorter working week. We were confident that we could do a big job by " direct action " and so were quite willing to let the other fellows play with the chase after parliamentary honours. This attitude to parliament and the failure to realize the need of continuous and consistent leadership embracing all phases of activity represented a fatal weakness that was to lead to our complete eclipse.

But while I refused to stand for parliament myself, I had no hesitation when approached by Gorbals Labour Party, in acting as " deputy " candidate for John McLean. The release of John McLean was one of the biggest issues before us and I took up this " deputy " position, supported by others, with the liberation of John McLean as the central question.

While these preparations were going on and just after we had celebrated the first anniversary of the Bolshevik Revolution, November 11 came and the war was at an end. I was out of Glasgow that day —in a train from Carlisle on the way to Barrow-in-Furness. There was relief and demonstrations in Glasgow, but it was nothing to what I saw in London when I arrived there for the one-day Labour Party Conference to which I was a delegate. The conference was called to discuss the question of a break with the Coalition. Clynes came to the conference with a message from Lloyd George pleading to keep the Labour Party in the Government. G. B. Shaw who was there made a characteristic speech, ending up with " Go back and tell Lloyd George—nothing doing." What a mean little fellow Clynes looked at that moment with all the delegates laughing at him. All those who had jobs in the Government spoke in favour of maintaining the coalition, but they were decisively defeated.

I made a short speech in which I attempted to show that the big question before us was the restoration of international solidarity and this task we couldn't possibly take up if we remained tied to the capitalist class. " Break with the enemies of the workers and join hands with our brothers of other lands."

If I had ended with this all would have been well, but I had to have a slap at J. H. Thomas, who in reply to something that had been said about revolution asserted that the only revolution he would stand for would be a peaceful revolution. I couldn't let this pass, and in the course of a few remarks about it, I said, " It's all very well to talk about a ' peaceful ' revolution, but when a revolution does come one of the strongest arguments will be a six-inch howitzer and the man at the business end of it is going to win the argument." This was blazoned all over the Press, nothing else mattered, and I became the recipient of the deep and heartfelt curses of many a well-meaning Labour candidate.

We also made a big agitation at this conference around the demand for McLean's release, helped very greatly by Robert Smillie who was then the leader of the miners.

The evening after the conference I was walking aimlessly about the Strand when I ran into Maxton. He persuaded me to go with him to a bit of a " do " down at the House of Commons. I think it was Joe King* who was giving it and all those who

---

* Joseph King, pacifist Liberal M.P. for N. Somerset (1910–18), who lost his seat in the Khaki election of the latter year, and joined the Labour Party.

represented what was supposed to be the " pacifist " section of the Labour Party were present. Mac-Donald (in the chair), Snowden, Smillie, W C. Anderson, Charlie Cramp and a crowd of others.

They had started eating when Maxton and I got in so we sat down near the foot of the table and applied ourselves to the job on hand. All those round about were delighted to see me, I couldn't get on with my eating for shaking hands. Then MacDonald got his eye on me. He came hurrying down, held out his hand and said in a voice of deep reproach, " You're a fine friend, Willie, to come in here and not shake hands with me." You see, he was depending on the support of the Glasgow men and if being nice to me was going to enable him to achieve his aim—well, he would be nice to me. In the same way if it was going to be to his advantage he would deal with me as his German colleagues dealt with so many, and exactly the same treatment would be meted out to anyone who was ever associated with him. His treatment of Morel was a classic example of his complete immunity from some forms of moral promptings.*

* When the 1924 Labour Government was formed it was generally expected that Morel, who was an authority on Foreign affairs, would go into the Foreign Office and there would pursue the policy of the Union of Democratic Control of which he was the leader. This was the last thing MacDonald wanted, so he approached Morel and told him a story about a non-existent conspiracy on the part of the trade union leaders to get one of their number into the post of Foreign Secretary. This he told Morel would be a complete barrier to the policy they were both interested in. He succeeded in insinuating into the mind of Morel that the

When the " bust " finished a group of I.L.P.'ers including the late Bruce Glasier, his wife Katherine, Kirkwood, Dick Wallhead, J. B. Houston, and several others, male and female, got me into their midst at Anderton's Hotel. They had booked a number of bedrooms there, several of which would be unoccupied, they had also a private sitting-room where we could have a chat before turning in. I went along and we all got comfortably settled in the sitting-room.

I had expected to have a talk on the workers' struggle, but Katherine got the floor and started off on transcendental religion. While she talked to them all, she seemed to single me out for special attention. The others kept trying to push me into a discussion with her, but I tried to keep out of it. She was talking a different language from mine and I knew we could never get on together. Unfortunately, after a bit I allowed myself to be jockeyed into it and I soon saw that my responses were causing the lady to open her eyes in shocked surprise. It was clear to her that I was sadly lacking in

---

only way to prevent such a catastrophe was for MacDonald himself to become Foreign Secretary as well as Prime Minister.

Morel, open and honest as the day, implicitly trusted the plausible MacDonald and followed up by coming out in support of him for Foreign Secretary.

It was not long before he realized the trick that had been played on him. It was a shattering blow to him when he found that his " colleague " had kept the Foreign Office safe for the old reactionary diplomacy. It is quite certain that this heavy disappointment had an injurious effect on his health, which wasn't too good. He died a few months later.

refinement. Nevertheless with quiet, self-subordin-
ating patience she laboured at her task. I must get
God. God was beauty and beauty was God and my
life was incomplete if I didn't have beauty.

" Take a rose," she said, " a rose is beautiful.
What gives it its beauty? It isn't its form. It isn't
its colour, it isn't the scent, it is something that is
inherent and gives rise to all these, that we call God
—so God is beauty—beauty is God." This was how
she argued.

I gazed at her in wonder. Then I said, " I think
I see what you're driving at."

She smiled, very sweetly.

I added: " Suppose you try it over again but
this time with a rotten egg."

She got up with great dignity and said in a cold
resigned voice, " Ladies, I think we'll retire." They
retired. My social debut was a complete and ghastly
failure—or was it?

Quite different appears to have been my evening
with Clare Sheridan. The advantage, moreover, in
this case was that I didn't happen to be there. This
lady, whom I have never seen, wrote a book in
which she spoke of old friends she had lost and
new friends she had found as a consequence of her
adventures amongst the Bolsheviks. One evening
a man came to her door. According to her description he looked a cross between a poacher and a
burglar. He introduced himself as Willie Gallacher,
the Clydeside revolutionary, so she bade him welcome. They spent a very pleasant evening together

and she thoroughly appreciated his visit. Whoever he was, I hope he didn't " touch " her for too much.

While we were in London Kirkwood and I visited the Labour Party headquarters and tried our utmost to get the official endorsement of McLean as the Labour candidate for Gorbals. Barnes had refused to accept the decision of the conference and was still in the Government, and was therefore finished so far as the Labour Party was concerned. But the leadership of the Labour Party would not yield.

" Anyone but McLean," they said.

We told them there would be no other. It was McLean or nobody. The local Labour Party was solidly behind him; why should they withhold their endorsement ?

McLean wasn't suitable.

Why wasn't he suitable?

Oh, he just wasn't suitable and beyond this we couldn't get.

We returned to Glasgow and redoubled our efforts for McLean's release. Lloyd George's coupon-holders couldn't get a hearing anywhere. No " toleration " for the Government representatives till McLean is back in Glasgow.

So fiercely was the campaign developing, the Government was forced to yield and on December 2, less than seven months after getting a five-years' sentence, McLean was released. That night when he arrived at Buchanan Street Station, we had a horse-drawn open carriage there to receive him. All round the station and down Buchanan Street was a crowd which literally packed the street. When the train drew in the cheering was terrific. With the utmost difficulty we escorted McLean to the carriage. The horse had been taken out and several of the stalwarts were in the shafts ready to start. But the difficulty of getting him through the crowd to the carriage was as nothing compared with getting the carriage out of the station and along the street. A huge red flag had been presented to him, and he stood in the carriage, a figure of revolutionary defiance, waving the flag above his head.

At a snail's pace we crept along amid deafening cheers. Crowds surged round the carriage and mounted it to shake hands with him or slap him on the back. Never in the history of Glasgow was there such a reception as John McLean got that night. By the time we got half-way down Buchanan Street the springs of the carriage had collapsed and the bottom was resting on the axles. We went across the river to Carlton Place, where after short speeches I got McLean away and we drove out to his home in a taxi. A week later the elections took place, and despite the opposition of the national Labour Party and the most unprincipled slanders on the part of the capitalist Press, McLean polled 7,436 votes on a revolutionary programme.

When the election was over we went down to Rothesay for a rest and a holiday, through the hospitality of Tom Anderson, one of the best known " old-timers " in Glasgow. He had a house there overlooking the front which he placed at our disposal. During this holiday it was apparent that McLean was getting into a very sick condition. He was seeing spies everywhere, suspecting everybody and anything. I tried my utmost then and subsequently to help him out of this condition, but unfortunately there were only too many ready to encourage him.

In 1920, when I was at the Second Congress of the Communist International, the comrades there all asked about McLean. Lenin especially was interested in him. He had a very high opinion of him and a very great regard for him.* When I told Lenin of his condition, he said: " You must get him to come over here. We will send him to one of our sanatoriums for a rest and he will soon be all right again. Many of our comrades have suffered the same way."

When I got back to Glasgow I went to see John and told him what Lenin had said about going over for a visit, without saying anything about treatment. He was agreeable to go as soon as he was finished

---

* Another gentleman who made a claim to Lenin's esteem is Mr. John S. Clarke. He wrote in an article published in a Scottish Sunday newspaper that Lenin, because of his great affection for him, which nobody else had noticed, had patiently taught his wife Krupskaya how to write a greeting in English on an autographed photograph for Mr. Clarke. I wrote to the editor of this paper and drew attention to the mendacity of this story. I pointed out that Krupskaya learned English before Lenin did and that twenty years before Clarke had visited Russia, Krupskaya had translated Webb's bulky volume on Trade Unionism from the English into Russian. Needless to say, the editor neither published nor acknowledged my letter.

with his immediate commitments. I thought everything was all right, but soon found my mistake.

There was a number of people around McLean at
this time, several of whom were actually living on
him. Never were there such monster meetings as
those which gathered round McLean; never such a
ready response with collections. Two or three of
these fellows went round with him all the time, and
drew a substantial salary out of it every week.
They set out to prevent him leaving Glasgow.
They had an able assistant in an S.L.P.'er who was
using him for another purpose.

When I discovered what was going on I went to
have a talk with John and found him changed
entirely. How did he know that I was telling the
truth about Lenin's invitation? Maybe I was
trying to get rid of him! I argued and argued with
him, but could not get him to decide. I went home
and wrote a letter to the S.L.P. Executive drawing
their attention to the serious state of McLean's
health, how he was suffering from hallucinations
and the serious consequences that would follow if
he did not get a rest and proper treatment. I explained my efforts to get him away and stated that
a member of their executive was primarily responsible for influencing him against going. I asked
them to allow me to talk to them in the presence
of this member, and above all to keep the contents
of my letter strictly confidential.

When the secretary of the S.L.P. got my letter he
immediately ran off a copy and sent it to the

member I had accused, asking him what he should do with it. The answer came back: send a copy to McLean. This was done, and the next thing I knew was that John was flourishing the letter on the public platform and declaring: "Gallacher wants to get rid of me, so he is circulating the story that I am mad."

It was impossible for me to do anything with him after that. I told the others they were driving him to his death, but they took no notice. Night after night they had him out in all kinds of weather, a sick man. After a bit his voice could scarcely be heard and his once sturdy body was shaken by a racking cough. But even when he could scarcely stand upright he was out in the streets, a bunch of toadies round him, battling for the revolution with his fiery spirit unquenched, but his body unable to resist the serious illness which had stricken him.

Coughing and choking, the dread malady of pneumonia laid its clammy hand upon him, and on November 30, 1923, the stormy life of John McLean, the Clyde's greatest revolutionary fighter, ended in the silent harbour of death.

CHAPTER X

THE BATTLE OF GEORGE SQUARE

IN January 1919 I returned from a short holiday at Rothesay, with a busy time ahead of me. Our factory movement had gained terrific strength and momentum, and we felt capable of tackling anything.

Every Saturday afternoon our delegates' meetings were packed, discussing hours and wages. A big discussion had taken place on whether we should organize action for a 30-hour or a 40-hour working week. There was no doubt in anybody's mind as to the possibility of securing action. We knew that all the intensive propaganda and agitation in the general fight against the War had prepared the way, and that all the principal factories were ready to move when the call was given.

So did the officials, with the result that a deputation, representing the Glasgow Trades Council and the trade union officials, came to our shop stewards' conference on Saturday, January 18, at which, with 500 delegates present, the call for action had to be decided. They asked to be allowed to participate in the strike call and in the leadership of the strike.

We gave them a welcome and then settled down to prepare the call and appoint a responsible leading committee. We appointed an equal number of officials and shop stewards on the committee, with two joint secretaries, Wm. Shaw, secretary of the Trades Council, and shop steward Dave Morton. Shinwell was made chairman of the joint committee, while I was appointed organizer of the strike.

The call issued from that meeting resounded along the Clyde and met with enthusiastic response everywhere.

" The Joint Committee representing the official and unofficial sections of the industrial movement, having considered the reports of the shop stewards and representatives in the various industries, hereby resolve to demand a 40-hour working week for all workers as an experiment with the object of absorbing the unemployed. If a 40-hour week fails to give the desired result a more drastic reduction of hours will be demanded. A general strike has been declared to take place on Monday, 24th January, and all workers are expected to respond. By order of the Joint Committee representing all workers."

I had to get round the factories, meet the shop stewards, and see that things were going the way we wanted. I had given up my job in order to devote myself to John McLean's parliamentary campaign in the Gorbals, so was now free to give all my time to the preparations for the strike.

One of my first tasks was to go to a mass meeting of Fairfield's workers in Govan and persuade them to return to work. They had made a sudden decision to strike on their own. After a short talk from me, supported by Tom Henderson, they unanimously decided to return to work and to come out with the others on January 27.

When the fateful day arrived the stoppage was practically complete. All the principal factories struck to a man. A mass meeting had been called for the morning of January 27 in St. Andrew's Hall. About 30,000 turned up for this meeting, which meant that with 3,000 inside we had about 27,000 outside. Fiery speeches were made and cheered to the echo inside and outside the hall. With unanimity, the following resolution was carried:

" That this mass meeting declares that no resumption of work will take place until the demand for a 40-hour week with no reduction of pay to time, piece or ' lieu ' workers has been conceded, and further that all negotiations for a settlement be made by or through the joint committee."

Instructions to the factory committee in whose areas one or two small factories were working to organize mass pickets and close them down, were followed by a report in the *Strike Bulletin* which we had arranged to have out in printed form every morning. After the meeting we formed up outside the hall and marched through the principal streets to George Square where we again spoke to the crowd that filled the square.

Marching with us from St. Andrew's Hall was our old friend Mrs. Reid, with her huge Red Flag. While we were speaking in the square, the flag was passed from hand to hand and then went flying aloft and gaily spread its scarlet folds from the municipal flag-pole. This, with the march, the singing, slogan-shouting and speeches, created an atmosphere of the highest tension and excitement. From Glasgow to London messages were flashing, suggesting possible happenings of all kinds. "Red Flag hoisted on municipal flag-staff"—what did it mean? Would we follow up with other action? This question was obviously agitating the minds of many people.

But for those of us who were leading the strike, we were strike leaders, nothing more; we had forgotten we were revolutionary leaders of the working class and while we cheered the flying of our flag, it had not for us the significant meaning it had for our enemies. They saw it as the symbol of an actual rising; we saw it as an incident in the prosecution of the strike. We were all agreed on the importance of the strike for the 40-hour week, but we had never discussed a general line against capitalism, and never could have agreed on it, even if we had discussed it.

Already the Press was being organized against us. The national officials of the unions were got at first. Edinburgh was out, so also was Belfast—to a man. But the national officials succeeded in holding back all the other areas, the A.S.E. executive even going so far as to suspend their Glasgow District Secretary, Harry Hopkins, from office for his participation in the strike committee.

We were being isolated and encircled with enemies, but we had possibilities of winning great new forces to our side if we had only the necessary revolutionary understanding and audacity. Revolt was seething everywhere, especially in the army. We had within our own hands the possibility of giving actual expression and leadership to it, but it never entered our heads to do so. We were carrying on a strike when we ought to have been making a revolution.

Well, we were determined to make the strike 100 per cent so far as the Clyde was concerned. So on Tuesday the mass picket took the field and covered the odd factory here and there where work was still going on. These pickets, five or six thousand strong, lined up at the factory gates, leaving a narrow channel which the workers had to pass through individually as they came out at the midday meal hour. No attempt at intimidation was made, no violence was at any time used, just the shouting of slogans " All out for the 40-hour week " and such similar calls. In every case, the workers coming out assured the picket that they also were in the fight, that they were not going back in. By Tuesday night or at latest Wednesday morning, every factory on the Clyde was shut down and sealed for the " duration." Our " strike bulletin " was going well and, selling at a halfpenny, we easily disposed of all we were able to print. During the brief period the strike lasted (little over two weeks) we made a profit of £193 10s. 2d. from the strike bulletin.

On Wednesday morning we had a mass demonstration to the Pinkston Power Station, just a try-out. We had not decided definitely just what we were going to do about such plants. From Pinkston we marched through the streets towards the centre of the city, George Square, where we meant the demonstration to disperse. On the way to the square, Shinwell, Hopkins and Kirkwood were in the lead. I was running up and down the line sorting out little difficulties here and there, trouble with the police and motorists, and so on. When I got to the square, Shinwell and the others had mounted the Gladstone Monument which stood where the War Memorial now stands, opposite the entrance to the municipal buildings. A great gathering in front of the Monument had already taken place, although the march into the square was still going on.

To my surprise, I discovered Shinwell was taking names for additional members to a delegation, the official representatives of which he had already announced. The deputation was going in to see the Lord Provost, for what purpose I wasn't clear, while I was to remain in charge of the demonstration. Cheered on by the enormous gathering the deputation, led by Shinwell, made its way into the headquarters of the civic authorities.

After about an hour the deputation came out. Shinwell reported having been received by the Lord Provost, and that the latter had promised to wire the Government on our demand for the 40-

hour week and had asked the deputation to come back on Friday for any reply that might come. We took it all in good faith and dispersed with agreement for another march on Friday, ending up in George Square, to hear the reply of the Lord Provost.

But it was obvious from the turn events took that the other side were making quite different arrangements. The reactionaries were away ahead of us. Unconscious of what was going on we dispersed to the districts the following morning, Thursday, the 30th, to make arrangements for a series of mass meetings throughout the area. At all these meetings the declaration to maintain the strike till victory was achieved, was reaffirmed. The spirit was wonderful. They were out to fight and out to win.

Following these meetings, we had a meeting of the strike committee at the office of the Glasgow Trades Council in Bath Street. At this meeting it was evident that apart from Edinburgh and Belfast we had failed to penetrate any of the other districts. From Barrow-in-Furness, the North-East Coast and Sheffield especially, we had expected action, but the national officials had succeeded in holding these and the other areas out of the fight.

Clearly it didn't look too good for us fighting alone on the Clyde with all the big industrial areas throughout England continuing at work, with the strong opposition of the national officials, with no strike benefit, added to all the Government and Press propaganda directed against us. We were faced with an exceptionally difficult situation. Then instead of us settling down to a political estimation of the task that confronted us, we were offered a number of romantic and dangerous suggestions from the chairman which would have ended everything in a medley of confusion and disorder. It was an unsatisfactory meeting from every point of view.

Propositions were put to me, which I didn't like but which I was prepared to carry out, and I demanded that a representative of the officials go along with me to share in whatever action we would have to take. Shinwell objected to this as they had so much work to do in connection with their unions.

Kirkwood intervened and declared, " Willie is right. If you want him to take responsibility for such actions as you propose, then someone has got to be there to share responsibility." That was Davie all over. However weak he might be politically his personal loyalty was never in question. In the same way when I was employed in Beardmore's at Mile End, I was summoned to the manager's office, arising out of a meeting I had addressed in the factory. When I got into the office, the manager was sitting at a table with the under-manager on one side of him and the cashier on the other. These three were backed up by all the principal foremen, one of whom happened to be Big Davie. It was an imposing-looking group. I pulled up a chair and sat down opposite the manager. He cleared his throat and then asked if I had said such and such a thing at the meeting. I countered this by asking if someone had told him I had said such and such a thing. He looked around at his henchmen and tried again. I said, " Look here, if you invited me up here to put me through a cross-examination you might have saved yourself the trouble. Produce your informant and I'll talk plenty; if you don't want to produce him the matter is finished. I make no answers. Is that clear? " Before he had recovered his breath Davie took the floor.

" What did I tell you," he shouted. " Didn't I tell you not to try it on? You thought you could frighten him. But Gallacher or me can never be frightened where our principles are concerned. We'll fight you to the death. Do you think we care for your job? We don't care that (snapping his fingers) for your job." The under-manager came around the table and whispered, " For the Lord's sake, Willie, get him out of here." So I got Davie out and we went back through the department with him loudly protesting all the way his opposition to tyranny and his determination to fight it to the death. How could I help having a soft spot for Big Davie?

When we finished a very inconclusive meeting of the strike committee I walked down Bath Street accompanied by J. M. Messer and Big Davie. Messer was very serious. The meeting we had just held had a very disturbing effect on him. He was convinced that the officials were looking for an opportunity of backing out of the strike.

" Shinwell wants to make trouble," Messer argued; " then he'll walk out and leave you to face the consequences."

To this I replied, " I can see what's going on all right. But I'm as smart as ever Shinwell was and if trouble comes I'll see that Shinwell's head goes below a baton before mine does."

Big Davie had a laugh at that one. " Man, you're an awful fellow," he remarked.

A bit self-confident I was, overmuch so. A little more political understanding and a little less self-complacency would have been an advantage to the workers who were looking for leadership. Think of it, the following day from 30,000 to 40,000 workers coming out on strike in answer to our call, and such was the condition of our leadership, no plan, no unity of purpose, watching one another and waiting for and wondering what was going to happen. It is not possible for the workers to understand in such circumstances. We were simply playing with the masses who were behind us, although we didn't stop long enough or think deeply enough to understand it.

So pleased was I with the " smartness " of this reply to Messer's serious warning, that when I got home I repeated it to my wife. She didn't laugh as Davie had laughed. She didn't think it so smart.

On the morning of Friday 31st, the Clyde district was early astir. From all parts of the area workers came pouring into George Square. Once again we made our platform the plinth of the Gladstone

Monument and from this, with one or two comrades up beside me, I addressed the huge gathering while the deputation headed by Shinwell and strengthened by Neil McLean, went in to see the Lord Provost.

The footpath and roadway in front of the Monument was packed with strikers. Down towards the post office at the south-east corner of the square there was a terrific jam. Lined up in front of the Municipal Buildings and therefore right up against the back of the strikers were several rows of policemen.

Suddenly, without warning of any kind, a signal was given and the police made a savage and totally unexpected assault on the rear of the meeting, smashing right and left with their batons, utterly regardless of whom or what they hit. Women and children were in the crowd, but this mattered nothing to these " guardians of the peace." With brutal ferocity, they made their onslaught on defenceless workers.

There was an immediate and irresistible surge forward and before those of us on the platform had time to grasp what had happened, the whole mass was rushing across towards the west side of the square, with the police maintaining their initial advantage of attacking from the rear.

Rain had fallen during the night and the square was wet and muddy. Men were sprawling all around; and just beneath where I was standing a woman was lying on her side and on her face were the marks of a muddy boot. This is absolutely true.

We all jumped off the plinth, and as the other comrades stooped to raise the injured woman, I ran across the square to where the Chief Constable was supervising the proceedings, surrounded by a guard of about ten policemen.

I rushed through before they were aware of my intentions. I had intended to speak to the Chief Constable and demand that he call off his men, but batons were raised all around me, so I struck out. I swung with all the power I had and landed on the Chief Constable. The only thing that saved me then was that too many tried to hit me at once and they got in one another's way. I managed to get in a "full power" uppercut which caught a constable right on the chin and nearly lifted his head off, before I was battered to the ground. I fell on my back and· with my hands pressed to the ground tried to raise myself. I saw the policeman I had hit with his baton in the air. He was going to smash my face in and I was too weak to get out of his way. Suddenly someone plunged and spread himself over the top of me; and the baton landed, not on my face but on the head of the comrade who had dived in to save me. He was dragged off me semi-conscious and I also was dragged to my feet. Blood was rushing from my head, all over my face and neck; and between blood and mud I was an awful spectacle. We were then half-dragged across the square towards the main entrance to the Municipal Buildings. I had a look at the comrade who had taken the blow that was meant for me.

I didn't know him. I hadn't seen him before, but I got to know him well during the trial that followed and through the succeeding years. He was Neil Alexander, a boilermaker, a quiet unassuming comrade, the type of worker who makes you feel that faith in the working class is founded on a solid rock.

Now a change was taking place on the west side of the square. After rushing across, the strikers were able to effect a right-about movement. No longer were their backs to the police, they were facing them and fighting back. They had them at a standstill. The noise was deafening and soon penetrated into the quiet of the Council corridor, where the deputation was patiently waiting for a Lord Provost who had no intention of seeing them.

One of the deputation looked out of a window and discovered to his horror that a battle was raging. This brought the whole deputation out with a rush. Kirkwood was at the front. He got out to the middle of the roadway just as I was being half-dragged towards the Council doorway. He raised his arms in a gesture of protest, when a sergeant, approaching him from the rear, brought down his baton with terrific force on the back of his head. Kirkwood fell flat on his face, unconscious. It was one of the most cowardly and unjustifiable blows I have ever seen struck. Neil McLean who was a pace behind Kirkwood, and who saw the vicious cowardly blow, rushed forward and protested strongly. If it had not been that they were a bit scared by the fact that he was a Member of Parliament, he would have got similar treatment. Kirkwood was picked up unconscious and carried through to the quadrangle of the Municipal Buildings, along with Neil Alexander and myself. Someone gave me a large piece of white cloth and I bound it around my head to stop the bleeding.

While I was standing thus my wife came through to see how I was faring. When she saw that I was all right, that I looked much worse than I really was, she let me have it. " What was that funny story you were telling me last night? " she asked. " The laugh's agin me," I answered.

Yes, the laugh was " agin " me, but it was going " agin " the police outside. Enraged beyond all bounds by the brutal and wanton attack that had been made upon them, the workers were still further infuriated as the word went round about the smashing that Kirkwood and I had received. With a roar of rage they rushed barehanded on the police and drove them back right across the square.

The Sheriff came out of the City Chambers with the Lord Provost and others and read the Riot Act.

When later on we were put on trial in the High Court in Edinburgh for inciting to riot and rioting, the police, one after another, swore that the trouble started with stone-throwing on the part of the strikers. Stones, chunks of iron, bottles, the air was black with them, all aimed at the police while they were still standing in front of the chambers and before they had made any attack on the strikers.

Yet the whole front of the City Chambers is one long series of windows, while out from the doorway there stand four medium high lamp-posts, each with a cluster of seven arc globes and not a lamp or a window was broken. Did this affect them in the " evidence " they were giving? Not a bit. Missiles, thousands of missiles, were thrown before they drew their batons.

Like well-trained parrots they kept on repeating what they had been taught to say, no matter how ridiculous it ultimately became. For here were photographs being taken after the demonstration had been broken up and the leaders arrested and those photographs show the whole roadway in front of the chambers, with the Sheriff and his cohorts, but not a sign, not the slightest vestige of a missile anywhere.

Were there missiles later on? There surely were. While the workers were driving the police back towards the east (the Council) side of the square, a big heavy lorry drove along, loaded with boxes of aerated waters. It was a gift from the gods. Some of the boys got hold of it and drove it into North Frederick Street, a street that rises on a high gradient from the north-east corner of George Square. With the utmost rapidity the boxes were piled up across the streets, piled up on their sides with the necks of the bottles ready to the hands of those who were manning the impromptu barricade. Foot police and mounted police tried to rush the barricade, but were driven back in disorder at every attempt. In the meantime the main body was closing in on the police across the square and forcing them right back into the Building.

Inside, we had been taken from the quadrangle into one of the corridors where we were able to sit down. We didn't know what was happening or how the fight was going, except that, in the early stages, workers were brought in hurt and bleeding to receive first aid or hospital treatment. Then after a bit, the workers ceased coming and policemen were carried in instead. We knew then that things were not going all the one way.

The police who were with us knew it too and they didn't look so good. Bailie Whitehead came along while we were sitting there and said " How are you feeling? " " Fine! " I replied. " Could I get you a glass of whisky? " he asked me. " No, thank you, Jimmy," I answered. " You know I never touch it." " I know, I know," he said, " but it wouldn't do you any harm just now." After a word or two more he went off, then the policeman who had tried to smash my face with his baton said, " You should have taken it, Willie, and gi'ed it to me." I looked at him. He was white and nervous. " By Christ," I said, " I believe you could do with it." " I could," was his frank reply.

But now the battle was coming near the chamber itself. We were removed from the corridor to a room upstairs, where we were shut in with several policemen. These policemen were glad to be out of it and were anxious to be on friendly terms with us. Anyone who wanted could get in to see us. The first visitors were Wheatley and Rosslyn Mitchell. Some remarks were made about our personal condition and then Wheatley informed us that we didn't have to worry about anything, that Mr. Mitchell would take charge of our affairs.

"Not mine," I said. "I've had some. I'll look after my own affairs and if I go to quod I'll know what I'm going for." That was the finish for me and Mr. Mitchell.

A few minutes later "Jock" McBain came in to see us with his head bandaged. He informed us that the police had been driven right up against and into the chambers. They wanted the crowd to march to Glasgow Green for a great protest demonstration there. But they wouldn't leave without word from us. "Would we go out and speak from the balcony?" This we eventually did, and the strikers formed up and marched off to Glasgow Green.

Had we been capable of planning beforehand, or had there been an experienced revolutionary leadership of these great and heroic masses, instead of a march to Glasgow Green there would have been a march to the Maryhill Barracks. For while troops, mostly young raw recruits, with tanks, machine-guns and barbed wire were being brought forward for the encirclement of Glasgow, the soldiers of Maryhill were confined to barracks and the barrack gates were kept tightly closed. If we had gone there we could easily have persuaded the soldiers to come out and Glasgow would have been in our hands.

That night Shinwell was arrested and during the following days Harry Hopkins, George Ebury of the B.S.P., young Brennan and several others were brought in. We were all taken to Duke Street Prison.

On the Saturday morning the troops marched with all the paraphernalia of war and took possession of the city.

The *Herald* for February 8 commenting on these developments said:

" The panic of the civic and national authorities can only be explained thus. They actually believed a Spartacus coup was planned to start in Glasgow, and they were prepared to suppress it at all costs."

This is correct. A rising was expected. A rising should have taken place. The workers were ready and able to effect it; *the leadership had never thought of it.*

All the London newspapers sent up special correspondents to write up the " revolt." They came in to find the military in control and the leaders of the " revolt " safe behind the bars. One of these special correspondents was Siegfried Sassoon, the young poet who, while showing exceptional bravery as a soldier, distinguished himself by his fierce hatred of and opposition to the war.

What an experience! There he was just a youngster, with all the desire of creative genius

surging up within him—in the midst of the " abom-
ination of desolation," mud and slime—and blood—
all churned up into an awful " Devil's Broth."
Destruction all around, destruction and death. Mad,
searing, shrieking death, while at home the mothers,
wives and sisters were poisoned by a continuous
stream of unholy lies about the glory of a "holy" war.
    From out of his scarred and wounded soul came
the cry:

> " O German mother dreaming by the fire,
>   While you are knitting socks to send your son,
>   His face is trodden deeper in the mud."

As I read that I had a vision of the mothers of all
nations searching the shell-torn battlefronts for their
children and as they gathered up the broken, tortured
bodies, they cursed in their bitter agony the criminal
gang that had sent their young to such a death.
    With intense hatred of the social system respon-
sible for the past black years, he came to Glasgow
ready to welcome a change whatever course it took.
    While in Duke Street Prison where we were
committed to await trial, bail having been refused,
I received a short note from Sassoon, dated February
7, which read:

" Dear Gallacher,
    " I was very sorry to have been unable to see you
yesterday. I should have enjoyed a talk with you—even
through a grating! Best of luck.
                    " Yours sincerely,
                        " Siegfried Sassoon."

He, like a good many others, was sadly disappointed at the turn of events. So many were not only expecting, but hoping, that a rising would take place in Glasgow.

A week later the strike was called off and the Clyde settled down to its normal life once more. Two weeks after that a Judge in Chambers granted bail of £300 for the principal leaders with lesser amounts for the others. When we came out of Duke Street Prison we found Glasgow still showing the " scars of war." All around the centre of the city, shop fronts were boarded up. Despite its short duration the fight had been a costly one.

The closing episode of the " revolt " took place in the High Court, Edinburgh, in the month of April, when Shinwell, Kirkwood, Hopkins, Ebury, Brennan, Alexander and myself came up for trial. I had decided to defend myself despite all efforts of the others to get me to accept Counsel. Of course all my colleagues on the Clyde Workers' Committee were with me in this decision. We had engaged Walter C. Leechman, the solicitor, an old member of the Labour Party, to assist us with legal advice and he proved eminently satisfactory.

At a meeting of the Counsel and clients held in Edinburgh a week before the court opened, reference was made to the fact that I was defending myself and the question was put by one of the K.C.'s (there were three of them, Watts, Sandeman and Constable), " Cannot you persuade him to accept Counsel? He'll probably ruin us all," to

which the answer was made, " No, he won't yield,
we've tried our utmost." One of the learned
gentlemen commented: " Maybe it's just as well,
a jury always like a scapegoat." This was taken
note of and duly reported by Leechman's Edinburgh agent who was present at the meeting.

It may be as well to say here that during the
course of the trial, none of the three K.C.'s made
any attempt to make me the " goat," but I mention
the incident to show the attitude of mind that is
held regarding juries and the character of their
judgment especially in political trials.

The night before the trial John Wheatley had a
talk with me. " I know you can face what is
coming," he said. He thought it was going to be
serious, and he was very anxious about Kirkwood.
" You know Davie better than anybody," he continued, " and you know how prison would affect
him." He wanted me to do everything possible to
get Davie out of it. This I readily promised. The
last man on earth I wanted to see going to prison
was Kirkwood. I knew what it was, and I knew
what it could do. To a man like Maxton, accustomed to moving around in an atmosphere of
happy-go-lucky friendship with all and sundry, it
had been a harsh nerve-racking ordeal faced with a
stout heart and a smile—however forced the smile
may sometimes have been.

For Johnny Muir it was a period of never-ending
agony. But if it was agony for Muir, what was it
going to mean for Kirkwood? Turbulent, dramatic,

he must always be expressing himself. He must always have an audience, be it one or a thousand. To shut such a man up is to kill him, to deprive him of all life's meaning. How he got through the three weeks in Duke Street Prison, without tearing the place to pieces, I don't know. I do know that he suffered terribly. He wanted to be out, to move about, to say and to shout aloud his hatred of capitalism and of all that it meant for the workers. Instead, shut in between bare walls, so close together as scarcely to leave room to breathe—a heavy iron-studded door—nerve-shattering silence.

The warder came into my cell one day to have a talk. He had just come from Davie's cell. " It's a shame," he said to me, " a big decent fellow like that in here. Prison is no place for him." Then he added, " It's different with you, Wullie, you're used to it." And what struck the warder is what will strike anyone who knows Big Davie. " Prison is no place for him."

Give him room and plenty of it. Let him talk and he'll talk plenty. Often he'll talk foolishly, but always he remains a big good-hearted proletarian, wandering these latter days sadly out of his depth, but nevertheless capable of getting back on the firm footing of the proletarian struggle once again.

The trial opened with a great array of witnesses for the prosecution, most of them policemen, but with the Sheriff of Lanarkshire and the Lord Provost of Glasgow thrown in.

The Counsel for the Defence riddled their evidence and I did my best to help. I was able to confuse certain police witnesses who testified against Kirkwood as to whether it was he or I who said the things they were charging him with and by this means shook them very considerably in the eyes of the jury.

When the case for the prosecution ended I suggested to the three K.C.'s that in view of the character of the evidence and the way it had been torn to shreds, we should close the case without bringing in defence witnesses. I was sure that if we addressed the jury on the evidence put forward they couldn't convict us. Counsel thought it advisable to have at least a few defence witnesses. Shinwell, Kirkwood and the others also wanted witnesses, and so it was decided. One of the defence witnesses almost sunk the ship with all hands aboard. He entered the box with a hard sullen look on his face. The Judge addressing him said, " Repeat after me, ' I swear by Almighty God——' "

" Whit God are yi talking aboot? " returned the witness.

The Judge drew himself up, then in a very stern voice: " Repeat after me, ' I swear by the Almighty God.' "

" Awa' wi yi'," returned the witness with an offensive look, " ye'r sittin' up there like a Punch and Judy in the Circus."

" Take that man away," commanded the Judge, and the police pulled him from the box.

Then Rosslyn Mitchell, who was solicitor for several of the accused, appeared as a witness for Kirkwood, Shinwell and Hopkins. Their Counsel examined him and he gave a glowing picture of their high and estimable characters. The Lord Advocate cross-examined him. In the course of the cross-examination, he asked him if he had heard me speak at the meeting on Wednesday, January 29. When he answered in the affirmative the Lord Advocate followed up by asking him what the character of the speech was, to which Mr. Mitchell answered that I was " very violent." " And did you consider it your duty as a public man to stand at such a meeting and listen to violent incitements without doing anything ? " questioned the Lord Advocate.

" I shouted out, ' Don't be a fool, Gallacher! ' " replied Mr. Mitchell.

" You don't have to worry," John Wheatley had said to me. " Mr. Mitchell will look after your affairs." Old John and I had many a laugh about that one afterwards.

At the conclusion Counsel addressed the jury on behalf of their clients. I listened in astonishment as they poured out their testimony to the virtues of the accused. If what they were saying was true then all those colleagues of mine had been doing the Jekyll and Hyde on me. " Gentlemen," said old Watts K.C., with a tremor in his voice, " look at him," pointing to one of the prisoners, " he's a Christian. His dear old mother who sits at home waiting for him, is a Christian. You cannot send a man like this to prison."

This was typical of the kind of appeal that was made for them. The Counsel had a job to do and they did it well. Their concern was to get their clients cut of it as expeditiously as possible. But some one had to take responsibility for the strike and the events that arose out of it, so I had to face the jury as the "villain of the piece."

In my address, I dealt with the strike and the demonstrations arising out of it. I justified all that we had done and then went on to deal with the attack by the police. I described the scene as I had observed it from the platform: how I jumped down to expostulate with the Chief Constable and the rush that was made at me by the police. " I am accused of having struck certain policemen," I said. " This part of the evidence is true. I struck out, I struck hard. My only regret is that I didn't have greater strength, so that I could have struck harder."

Following this I went on to declare my determination to keep at the fight whatever happened, ending with " Gentlemen, it is for you to decide. You can decide that I'll sleep to-night in my own home or in a prison cell, but believe me, which ever it is, I'll sleep with an easy conscience."

The Judge, Lord Scott Dickson, then summed up and practically wiped out the charge against Kirkwood, Hopkins, Ebury and Alexander. At the conclusion he took occasion to say: " One thing the

Court must take note of, Mr. Gallacher has played the game by his colleagues."

The jury decided without loss of time for a verdict of " not guilty " on all prisoners with the exception of Shinwell and me. Against Shinwell there was no evidence but an abundance of prejudice for which the prosecutor had been responsible. They argued long about Shinwell and then decided to find him " guilty." About myself there was also a long argument, several of the jurymen were disposed to be lenient but they couldn't get over the fact that I had struck the Chief Constable. This was decisive. I also was slated " guilty." Shinwell was sentenced to five months' imprisonment, I got off with three. After shaking hands with Kirkwood and the others who now left the dock free men, I turned to where my wife was sitting in the Court, accompanied by Wheatley, waved my hand and said, " I could do it on my head." This was more to reassure my wife than with any sense of bragging.

Thus ended the " war " struggle of the workers of the Clyde.

.   .   .   .   .

We continued to carry on for several years, with the reappearance of the *Worker* as our central organ. We had now as one of our leading figures J. R. Campbell, who had been discharged from the Army early in 1918, bearing with him a lifelong reminder of war and its havoc. As a boy he had been a keen member of the old S.D.P. and later the B.S.P. Now with all his war experience he threw himself into the struggle and soon became one of the foremost leaders of the factory movement.

But however effective our factory work might be, and in many directions it was undoubtedly good, we failed entirely to develop any effective general line and so the general leadership of the movement passed more and more into the hands of the reformists.

In 1918 we had marched through Glasgow on May 1, 100,000 strong. On May 1, 1924, Harry McShane, one of McLean's best and most loyal lieutenants, and I led a demonstration through the street—100 was our full muster.

The reformists had succeeded in sapping the revolutionary movement for the time being. We were down to zero. But that 100 was the first attempt at a May Day demonstration since 1918. It was a start and from it we have gone and will continue to go forward.

While we were preparing the campaign for the shorter working week, we were approached by a deputation of blind workers employed at the Royal Blind Asylum for a special form of assistance.

These blind workers engaged in all kinds of basket and mat work, were receiving wages that scarcely kept body and soul together. The institution was maintained by a voluntary subscription much of which came from the factories, while a considerable amount came from rich and petty-bourgeois sympathizers.

At the beginning of the year an annual meeting of the subscribers was held at which the board of directors was elected. A deputation from the blind workers wanted me to attend the subscribers' annual meeting and they would guarantee my election on to the board with the responsibility of getting a general all-round increase of wages.

Although I had many other commitments the boys were all of the opinion that I should accede to this request and make a fight to change the conditions in the institution. Accordingly I attended the subscribers' meeting and was duly elected on to the board of directors. I was unable to attend a meeting until my release from prison. When I did attend, I found myself in a very select and respectable company. There was a baronet and several other very pronounced " gentlemen," including a couple of clericals, several ladies, and a group of Labour men headed by Willie Shaw, secretary of the Glasgow Trades Council.

After routine business was finished I raised the question of wages and proposed an all-round increase of 50 per cent. I have never known such abundant sympathy as was expressed by those ladies and gentlemen, but—where was the money to come from? A general doleful shaking of heads at this. I said I wasn't at the moment discussing where the money was to come from, but where what money we had was going, and I was certain there wasn't enough of it going to the blind workers. Well, we had an awful row, and the meeting broke up without a decision.

The next meeting found them prepared. They brought in the superintendent, a large well-kept gentleman who supplied us with a mass of figures, a favourite trick of company promoters and of a certain type of " kept " trade union officials. These figures all went to show that out of the money that came from various sources, this had to be paid, that had to be paid, the next thing or the other had to be paid, and so it was plain for all to see that there was nothing left with which to raise wages. I said, " I don't like this way of dealing with the question. Let us try it the other way. Out of whatever money is coming in, we'll raise wages, then if there is anything left, we'll pay for this, that and the other."

All of them looked aghast. They had never before heard of a proposal so directly in opposition to their accepted mode of thinking. One and all declared it was bad economy and could not be supported. " Bad economy "—starve the workers, blind or sighted, that's always good economy, always arguments will be found to justify it, but pay the workers—out come the figures. It can't be done, it's " bad economy."

But while they had been declaring the figures we had been making a campaign and I now threatened them with mass demonstrations if the blind workers weren't considered first and so the wage increase was forced through, much against the will of the board members.

I then paid a visit to the institution and made a thorough examination of its character. There was a superintendent with £950 or thereabouts a year, then an assistant superintendent with £400 a year, in the factory itself a blind foreman who did all the practical work.

After going very carefully into the matter I made a proposal at the next meeting of the committee that almost shook my co-directors out of their chairs. I proposed the dismissal of the superintendent and the assistant superintendent and the appointment of a man at £500 a year to replace them. Did we have a fight? I can say we did. Such nice ladies and gentlemen, always anxious for economy, when it affects the workers; but a nice Christian gentleman like the superintendent, a top-hatted, frock-coated pillar of the Church is different. It was monstrous. But monstrous or no, it had to go through.

The superintendent and his assistant got a month's notice and an advertisement appeared in the Press, offering the post of superintendent to a competent man at £500 a year. Believe it or not, the superintendent who for years had been drawing round about £950 a year, while the blind workers went short, put in an application for the job at £500 a year, so also did the assistant. When the latter was in before the board I asked him if he agreed with the observations I had made in connection with the institution, and with the conclusion I had drawn

that one man could do the job. " Yes," he replied,
" I am in complete agreement. As a matter of
fact, I do everything now, the superintendent does
nothing."

Out of the money that came in, this sort of thing
had to be paid for before the blind workers could
get anything. What applied there applies in greater
or lesser form to every other institution and every
industry in the country.

CHAPTER XI

WHEN I came out of prison in July 1919 I immediately started in search of work. Morning after morning I went the round of the Clyde workshops, but all in vain. I was " black-listed," and for a long time I couldn't find a foreman prepared to take a chance. Then at last I met one at Binnie's at Cordonald. He said he would risk giving me a job and started me on a heavy horizontal boring machine. I used to go in bright and fresh in the morning and come out old, worn and tired at night.

But it didn't last long. The day after I got started I took another Paisley engineer along with me and he also got a job. We were working a week when the managing director appeared on the scene with the manager. They came into the shop and, a short distance from where I was working, had an angry session with the foreman. When they finished the foreman came over to me and said,

" I'm sorry, Willie, I tried to save you, but it was no use. You've got to go, you and your friend." The two of us went but alas, not alone. The foreman got the " sack " along with us. He had held the job for years, but was given a month's wages in lieu of notice and cleared out on the grounds of " incompetence."

The story went flying round the Clyde. If the foremen had been shy of me before, it was nothing to their attitude now. They'd cross to the other side of the road if they saw me coming and hurry as fast as their legs would take them. They were afraid to be seen speaking to me even though it were to curse me. Hitherto I had never taken a fee of any kind for speaking, in fact I had created quite a sensation while I was in America by refusing a fee. Everybody got paid, from a humble couple of dollars up to 100 or 150 dollars a speech. I spoke many times in America but never at any time took a cent. But early in 1920, I had to rely on the comrades and they were ready to stand by. I got small fees for the various campaigns in which I took part and was able to get along.

Early in 1920 the question of unity and the formation of a Communist Party in Britain as a section of the Third International was being widely discussed and already considerable advances had been made by certain parties and groups of parties. These comprised the B.S.P., a strong section of the S.L.P. including its foremost leaders, Sylvia Pankhurst's group around the *Workers Dreadnought* and a group of Left I.L.P.'ers.

But while these were negotiating in London, the movement was taking a different course in Glasgow and in other parts of Scotland.

The shop stewards movement had a strong antiparliamentary bias, while the Glasgow S.L.P. was violently opposed to its own leaders associating with the B.S.P. Associated with them was a group formed around John McLean, who had broken from the B.S.P. and was now pursuing a course of his own.

Amongst all of these the idea of a Scottish Party free from the opportunism and corruption that was —rightly or wrongly—associated with London, rapidly gained ground.

I had been invited to attend the second congress of the Communist International as the representative of the Clyde shop stewards, and in July 1920 I left for Moscow. As I had no passport, I had to get in touch with a comrade in Newcastle in order to be " put wise " for smuggling myself aboard a Norwegian boat. Without a passport I could not travel as a passenger. I had to travel as a stowaway. I had a week hanging about the Newcastle docks before I succeeded, with the help of a fireman who was a party comrade, in stowing myself safely away on a ship bound for Bergen. Six hours before the ship sailed I was aboard and I counted every minute of it always expecting to be dragged out and handed over to the police. From Bergen, with the assistance of the party there, I sailed as a passenger to Vardo and from there in a little motor fishing boat, across a strip of the Arctic Sea to Murmansk. From Murmansk I went to St. Petersburg (now Leningrad) where the Congress had to open, but by the time I got there the opening had already taken place and the congress had moved on to Moscow. With little delay I got to Moscow and was soon engaged in discussions which completely altered my views on revolutionary politics.

But this change did not take place in any easy manner. At that time the shop stewards' movement was still comparatively strong and I had little regard for parties and still less regard for parliament and parliamentarians. I was an outstanding example of the " Left " sectarian and as such had been referred to by Lenin in his book *Left-Wing Communism, an Infantile Disorder.*

But here I was in the company of Lenin himself and other leading international figures, arguing and fighting on the correctness or otherwise of these views. I was hard to convince. I had such disgust at the leaders of the Labour Party and their shameless servility that I wanted to keep clear of contamination.

Gradually, as the discussions went on, I began to see the weakness of my position. More and more the clear simple arguments and explanations of Lenin impressed themselves in my mind. When I got back to Glasgow I tried to give the comrades some idea of how I felt when talking with Lenin. I had never had such an experience with anyone before. Here was a man on whom the eyes of the world were turned. A man who was making history, great history, yet simple, unaffected, a true comrade in the deepest meaning of the word. Not for a moment could I dream of talking about him—to him.

I couldn't even think of him when he was talking to me. The remarkable thing about Lenin was the complete subordination of self. His whole mind, his whole being, was centred in the revolution. So when I spoke to Lenin, I had to think not of him, but of what he was thinking—about the revolutionary struggle of the workers.

Occasionally in the discussions taking place in the various Commissions Lenin would scribble a note clearing up a particular point and pass it to this or that comrade. One evening in the hotel I was commenting on the caustic character of such a note he had passed and how certain people would go red in the face if they had seen it.

" Where is it ? " asked J. S. Clarke.

" I tore it up," I replied.

" What! " he exclaimed. " You tore up a note in Lenin's handwriting ? "

" Yes," I said, " I have torn up several. I always tear up whatever notes I have at the end of a sitting."

" If you get another, keep it and give it to me," said Clarke.

The next day I happened to make a heated reference to the criticism in *Left-Wing Communism* and Lenin passed me a note which read: " When I wrote my little book I did not know you." I kept that one but gave it to Clarke. He now writes fantastic stories about his relations with Lenin.

The more I talked with Lenin and the other

comrades, the more I came to see what the party of the workers meant in the revolutionary struggle. It was in this, the conception of the party, that the genius of Lenin had expressed itself. A Party of revolutionary workers, with its roots in the factories and in the streets, winning the Trade Unions and the Co-operatives with the correctness of its working-class policy, a party with no other interests but the interests of the working class and the peasant and petty-bourgeois allies of the working class, such a Party, using every avenue of expression, could make an exceptionally valuable parliamentary platform for arousing the great masses of workers to energetic struggle against the capitalist enemy.

Before I left Moscow I had an interview with Lenin during which he asked me three questions.

" Do you admit you were wrong on the question of Parliament and affiliations to the Labour Party ? "

" Will you join the Communist Party of Great Britain when you return ? "

(A telegram had arrived a couple of days before, informing us of the formation of the Party.)

" Will you do your best to persuade your Scottish comrades to join it ? "

To each of these questions I answered " yes." Having given this pledge freely I returned to Glasgow.

On arrival I heard of a conference that had been held two weeks previously, when the question had been discussed of forming a Scottish Communist Party, compounded of the sectarians of the S.L.P., the shop stewards and the Scottish nationalism of the group round John McLean. I also heard that a further conference was to take place on the Saturday following my return, to elect an Executive Committee and to launch the Communist Party officially.

On the Saturday I was at the hall where the conference was being held and asked to be allowed to make a statement before the delegates took any final decision. This was generally agreed to, although there was some opposition from the Glasgow S.L.P. representatives.

I made a short report of the discussions at the Second Congress and went on to explain the case that had been put by Lenin. I ended up by advising the delegates not to go ahead with the formation of a party or the election of an executive but to elect a provisional committee, responsible for opening unity negotiations with the recently formed Communist Party of Great Britain.

This met with fierce protests from a few of the S.L.P.'ers but after a short discussion was accepted by the overwhelming body of delegates present. A provisional committee was elected but, not being a delegate, I could not be elected on to it. This difficulty however was overcome by the conference empowering the committee to co-opt me in an " advisory capacity."

Negotiations were immediately commenced and as a result a unity conference was held in Leeds early in January 1921, and the Scottish comrades were absorbed in the C.P.G.B.

At this unity conference it was agreed to make new elections for President of the party (a post that has long since disappeared) and the executive. Arthur McManus was already President of the C.P.G.B. and was of course nominated again. The Scottish comrades, although they had much less voting power than the already established C.P.G.B., insisted on putting me forward for this position. My nomination went forward against Arthur but he was re-elected by a very large majority. Nominations for the executive had to go in at the same time as nominations for President, Secretary and Treasurer and as the rules laid it down that no member could be nominated for two positions, I was not nominated and therefore could not be elected to the Executive. I remained a " rank and filer.''

At this time the Miners' campaign was in the forefront of the working-class struggle. I was agitating continually throughout Lanarkshire and Fife. The big question was " would the Triple Alliance " (miners, railwaymen and transport workers) function, would the railwaymen and transport workers fall in behind the miners? A short while after the unity conference, I went to fulfil an engagement in Birmingham, and then go on to Liverpool. At the Birmingham meeting another old comrade of mine from Glasgow was present, one of the most fiery and dramatic of all our propagandists. On the conclusion of my speech, the chairman invited this comrade, who was sitting in the audience, to say a few words, which he did with a vengeance.

There were three C.I.D. men present and he centred attention on them. He had that audience shouting, in a wild frenzy. A week later in Liverpool I was arrested and held in custody till an officer from Birmingham came to take charge of me. This officer was a very pleasant fellow and informed me on the way to the station that he was a relative of a prominent leader of the Labour Party. When we got seated in the train there were two other people in the carriage, a young man on my side of the carriage and an elderly man on the other with my custodian. We talked about the miners, then about Germany and about Russia. The elderly gent was a great listener and keen to hear about other places and other countries. He said to me with a note of envy in his voice, " You appear to have travelled quite a lot." " Oh, here and there," I replied.

He looked at me with a wistful smile. " Maybe you are travelling somewhere now? " he suggested.

" I am," I replied, " and I'm likely to be away for quite a while." I'm quite sure he would have given all he had to be in my place at that moment.

The train pulled up, at Stafford I think, and the officer said, " Come out and have a cup of tea, Willie." Out we went. We had to go back quite a way along the platform to get to the refreshment room. The officer ordered tea and a bun for me and a bottle of stout for himself. While we were in the middle of it the whistle blew and the train began to jerk. " Come on, Willie," the officer shouted and off he went, rushing out of the buffet and along the platform. I went tearing after him. The train was already making way as he pulled open a door and jumped in, a porter made a rush with the intention of stopping me, but I beat him to it. I got into the corridor and found the officer squatting on his haunches trying to get his breath back. I squatted beside him. Suddenly he looked at me and exclaimed: " My Christ, Willie, what would have happened to me if you hadn't got the train? "

" There would have been no sense in me lying back," I told him. " I couldn't go into hiding without being lost to the movement, so I may as well face what's coming and get it over."

" Well, you've saved my job," he replied.

The next morning I came up before the court and got an adjournment for a week, on bail. Back in Scotland I got a letter from the Party centre informing me that arrangements had been made for W. H. Thompson, the solicitor, to meet me in Birmingham and assist in preparing my defence. I was advised to meet him in the Station Hotel the night before the case came up. I did so and found that he had booked a double bedroom for the night. It turned out to be an enormous room with two large beds, easy chairs, desks and all the rest of it. It looked real good but when he told me it cost a pound a head for room and breakfast, that finished me. I scarcely slept all night thinking about it.

In court the next day Lord Ilkeston occupied the bench. I have met many friendlier men in my time, but few less so. The indictment accused me of sedition while speaking at a Communist meeting in the Bristol Street School. I took objection to this and produced a leaflet advertising the meeting as being held under the auspices of the National Shop Stewards and Workers' Committee Movement.

The prosecutor said this was a branch of the Communist Party (he had forestalled Citrine's solar system). I showed that the Communist Party had only come into existence the previous August and that the Shop Stewards Movement had been active for several years, that therefore the contention of the prosecutor was absurd. It was no use. My objection was overruled. But worse was to follow.

The prosecutor after quoting several learned opinions on sedition, said that I had made a very clever but a very careful speech. This speech, however, he went on, had to be taken in conjunction with another speech, made directly after mine and for which my speech had prepared the way. He did not propose to quote from my speech as there was no particular passage that could be used by itself. The speech had to be considered as a whole and in the light of what followed after. He then called one of the C.I.D. men, a shorthand-writer and asked him to read out the other fellow's speech.

Again I objected. I said I was prepared for consideration to be given to what I had said myself but that I was not responsible for anyone who might have been called to the platform after I had spoken. Objection overruled. They were determined to get me. The wildest passages from my colleagues' speech were then read out and the case continued, concluding with the genial Lord Ilkeston deciding that I was guilty and imposing on me a sentence of three months.

Thompson wanted me to appeal but we had in our party at that time certain " leftist " objections against appealing to a capitalist court, so despite all his urging I refused although he was convinced that I would have won on either of the points I had raised.

While in Winson Green prison, I heard of the manner in which Frank Hodges had betrayed the miners' cause at a meeting of M.P.'s held in the House of Commons, of how this provided an excuse for Bevin and Thomas to break up the Triple Alliance and leave the miners isolated. I used to pace the cell at night wishing I was out and I cursed myself for not having taken the opportunity of appealing in view of the strong case I had.

While in Winson Green I met a young chap who had just come in with a sentence of eighteen months. He had been a bank clerk in Coventry. Towards the end of 1917 many bundles of notes paid out to one of the big Coventry firms for the payment of wages, were found to contain, except for the top and bottom notes, Bible leaves. £3,000 had gone astray. Where it had gone or who was responsible could not be discovered. In 1918 the young bank clerk was called up. After training he did a short term in France, then the war ended. He was demobilized about the end of 1919. He got his job back in the bank but could not settle down to it. This led to continual trouble between him and the bank manager.

About the end of 1920 things got so bad that the manager appealed to the directors to have him transferred. It was decided to transfer him to a small country branch. Before he left he had a row with the manager, his final words being: " I'm glad I did you in in 1917."

That put the manager on the scent. Straight to the police he went. New inquiries were started and the thefts were traced to this young bank clerk. I have often heard it said that criminals are discovered because they cannot refrain from bragging of their deeds. This was certainly a striking proof of such an assertion.

When I finished my three months' sentence I made a short visit home and then made my way to Fife to take a hand in the miners' strike which was then well under way. I was met at Cowdenbeath station by a demonstration of several thousand miners with a band at their head.

We marched along the main street to Stein Square where a most enthusiastic meeting was held. This was followed up by meetings in most of the other villages, all of them, to the very end of the strike, of a most militant and high-spirited character.

Very few of those who took an active part in the movement at that time remain in it to-day. A notable exception is Jimmy Stewart of Lochgelly.

He was one of the most loyal and hard working of our comrades then, he remains the same loyal and hard-working comrade to-day. In 1921 he went on a miners' delegation to Russia. In a train smash there, in which a Welsh comrade was killed, Jimmy met with a serious accident and was detained for a considerable time. But as soon as he got back he was in the thick of the struggle again.

During 1921 things were not going too well with the party. The post-War revolutionary wave had created widespread support for the revolutionary movement, all kinds of people were helping financially and this attracted every variety (and there were many) of political adventurers.

Some of these had bounced their way into the leadership of the newly formed Communist Party and into control of its paper *The Communist*. While up in Scotland I was asked to write an article for the paper. I did so. My article was a column and a half long. The following week I received a letter which read as follows:

" Mr. W. Gallacher,
" Dear Sir,
    " Enclosed please find postal order for 31s. 6d. being payment for your article in the *Communist*.
                                  " Yours, etc.,
                                  ————

I could scarcely believe my eyes. I looked at it in a kind of daze. My wife asked me what was wrong. " Look," I said, handing her the letter.

She looked at it, then looked at me. " Well, you know what to do," she said; " send it back." I wrote a few lines which read:

" Dear Sir,
    " When I wrote my short article for the *Communist* I wrote it as a Communist, which I am, not as a journalist, which I am not.
" Yours, etc.,
" Wm. Gallacher."

I pinned the postal order to it and sent it off. That started a fight for a clean-up in the party. When the fight ended that man and a whole lot more of his kind had gone, in search of more lucrative fields than the Communist Party was prepared to offer. During the period of this fight the party headquarters were raided. Albert Inkpin, the party secretary, was arrested, and Arthur McManus the party president, worked away from the office. This called for someone to take charge at headquarters. Tommy Clark, who had been odd-jobbing about the place for some time, was given the responsibility. For years he had posed as a " great revolutionary leader." This on the strength of his De Leonite recitations in the days before the War. Now he was given a chance to show what he could do. He showed that he could do nothing. Never was there a greater flop. The party could do no other than get quit of him with the utmost dispatch. But the comrades could not bring themselves to believe that one who had carried around such a reputation could be so worthless as he appeared to be. They thought maybe he was out of his element in London, so they gave him a job in the Glasgow office. There it was the same thing. The rawest recruit to the party would have been more use than he was. He went out of the Glasgow office conscious of his own complete failure and as a consequence with the seeds of an undying hatred against the party that had called and exposed his bluff.

Willie Paul and others held things together till McManus was able to return to the office and take up the threads again. But still there were many difficulties to be faced and overcome. Tommy Bell was in Moscow working hard in the Communist International and could not easily be spared from there. The Executive therefore took a decision to co-opt me and to make me Vice-President of the party in order to help get it out of the confusion it was then in. This brought me down to London in time to take part in the preparations for the St. Pancras Congress of the Party. For this Congress the political adventurers were making special preparations in order to keep their paralysing control over the party.

The night before the Congress they had organized a fraction meeting to which they had invited a number of good party delegates whom they hoped to trick into supporting the line they intended to take. One of these was the same comrade who spoke with me in Birmingham. It was all done in the utmost secrecy but they made a mistake in the choice of this particular comrade for he immediately came to me and advised me as to what was going on. Their consternation when I walked into their meeting may be imagined.

They tried to put as good a face on it as possible, but after a very few words I got all the delegates present to understand the game that was being played and persuaded them all to leave the meeting.

The next two days saw the complete discomfiture of all of this particular type of " Communist " and it wasn't long before the party was quit of them for good and all.

But while most of them just faded away without a sound and without leaving the faintest trace behind, there was one who felt he had to make a splutter. This was a gentleman since a Labour M.P. For quite a time, while the revolutionary tide was high, he had gone dashing around Russia and Germany until he hypnotized himself into the belief that he was " redder " than a boiled lobster.

But when his wild journeyings were ended and he had to face up to party membership and party responsibility in England, there was a different story to tell.

He wrote a letter to our party headquarters extolling in the most fulsome language the Communist Party of Russia and the Communist Party of Germany. With such parties as these, it was in keeping with the dignity of an English gentleman to be associated, but with the British Party! If it hadn't been that he was so well brought up he'd have spat when he mentioned the name.

Not for him the British Party, until it was of the calibre of the Russian or German Parties. I remember writing him a reply starting with the well-known lines:

"I do believe in Freedom's Cause, as far away as Poland is."

and going on to expose the humbug and pretence of his " Bolshevism."

He was like many others. If those of us who were labouring to build a party succeeded in our efforts and the party became a force in the country, then they would graciously condescend to join. But the party that is strong enough to attract them, will also be strong enough to keep them out.

After the miners' strike ended, trouble broke out in the Fife, Kinross and Clackmannan Miners' Union, the secretary of which was the Right Honourable William Adamson*. Away back in the early days of Labour representation it was decided to contest West Fife, and Robert Smillie was the almost unanimous selection. Adamson tried by every means to get this decision overturned. He failed, but he made his determination to run as an independent so clear that Smillie wrote to the com-

---

* Mr. Adamson has died since this was written, passing away in a Dunfermline nursing home on February 23, 1936.

mittee and withdrew his name, explaining that he
didn't want to see the Fife Miners' Union split on
such an issue. A close friend of the coalowners and
of every Tory in Fife and out of it, Adamson had to
have his own way, or he would split the union.

Thus, out of the fight for the reform of the union
which followed the 1921 strike, there developed a
split and the formation of a Reform Union, brought
about by the stubborn resistance of Adamson to
any democratic change being made.

The secretary of the new union, Philip Hodge,
ran as an Independent Labour candidate at the 1923
General Election, but he didn't prove very satisfactory and the young men who were the active
spirits in the Reform Union campaigned for a new
candidate.

As I was well known throughout Fife and had
taken part in so many of the struggles an approach
was made to get me as candidate. I had however
been previously adopted for Dundee where I had
contested in 1922 and 1923. The first time I got
six thousand odd votes, and the second time my vote
went up to over ten thousand.

By 1934, however, the Fife boys were campaigning within the party to get me transferred to Fife.
So hotly was the matter being contested that in
the election of 1924, the one following the defeat
of the Labour Government, I didn't stand at all.
Following this election the decision was taken to
transfer me and I was allocated to West Fife as the
prospective parliamentary candidate.

In 1925 I was a delegate to the Liverpool Labour Party Conference. During the discussion on the expulsion of the Communists, I drew attention to the fact that the conference was proposing to exclude some of the best working-class fighters, and the men who were inciting the conference to this course were the leaders who were continually wining and dining in the camp of the enemy.

A little later Aitken Ferguson and I met Mac-Donald and Tom Johnston in one of the corridors. MacDonald said: " I hope you were not referring to me, when you spoke of the leaders wining and dining in the camp of the enemy."

" I was," I replied.

" Then it's not right, Willie," he pleaded in his most suave manner, " I don't believe in all this banqueting that goes on. I may go to Buckingham Palace or Balmoral Castle now and again but you can't call that the camp of the enemy."

I said, " Are you trying to have a joke at my expense? Maybe you'll tell me next that it's all workers you meet there." He got a bit nettled at my tone and responded somewhat sharply:

" You don't know anything about what goes on there, so you shouldn't talk."

" I know all right," I said.

" You don't," he asserted, adding: " I'll tell you what I'll do, I'll take you to Balmoral Castle the next time I go and let you see for yourself."

Yes, sir! that was big, brave, handsome Mac.

" All right," I informed him, " I'll go, and I

won't misconduct myself. I'll behave as I behave
with the boys in the workshop or at the street
corner and I'll bet I don't get invited again, and
neither will you for having taken me."

That finished J. R. M. He went off in a huff.
He didn't take me to Balmoral. Joynson Hicks got
in before him and took me to Wandsworth prison,
with another eleven of the Communist party leaders
to keep me company.

The Labour Party leadership succeeded, through
the decisions of the 1925 conference, in isolating us
from the general body of the workers, and the
Baldwin Government, as part of its preparations for
the attack on the miners, followed up with our arrest
and imprisonment. As early as 1925 MacDonald,
Thomas and Co. were working in close combination
with Baldwin against the revolutionary advance of
the working class.

When the great strike of 1926 took place, I was
in Wandsworth prison. I had felt impatient in
Birmingham, but I was worse in Wandsworth.

I longed to be out and to have the opportunity
of participating in the strike activity. We got some
news inside but only of the scantiest and most disconnected kind. But one thing was clear. The
classes were in open confrontation. The capitalists
and their lackeys looking to and taking orders from
the Baldwin Government, the workers looking to
and taking their orders from their own government
—the General Council. I knew that such a situation
could only last for a very short time. I wrote out a

statement for discussion (on toilet paper) in which
I laid down three possible solutions:

1. The Baldwin Government would arrest the
General Council, declare the Strike illegal, and
proceed to suppress it.
2. The General Council would arrest the
Baldwin Government, would declare for a Workers' Republic and proceed to suppress the bourgeoisie.
3. The General Council would make a complete capitulation and betray the working class.

This last I pointed out, was the solution the
General Council would inevitably take. A class
action such as was in progress then demanded a class
leadership, a leadership that had not been corrupted
by, and made part of, the bourgeoisie.

Such a leadership we had to try and get in face
of the imminent betrayal of the strike. This
leadership alas had not yet been hammered out and
steeled on the anvil of experience and so the great
betrayal took place. But a new confrontation will
take place, this time with the lesson of 1926 well
learned—a class leadership for class action and
victory is assured.

CHAPTER XII

AFTER THE GENERAL STRIKE

WHEN I came out of prison in the month of September I went off for a short holiday. I was reluctant to go but the party leadership had decided that the twelve of us should follow this course to give us an opportunity of studying the developments that had taken place while we were away. At the end of my holiday I went to the Durham area where a week's campaign had been organized for me.

As soon as I reached Durham the Home Secretary, the late Sir William Joynson Hicks, issued a warrant under the Emergency Powers Act, prohibiting me from organizing or speaking at any meeting in the county of Durham. All the time I was in the county the police were chasing after me in a couple of taxis, much to the amusement of the miners.

But I was able to circumvent them with the assistance of the miners' lodge officials. Mass lodge meetings were held and in the midst of the business I would appear on the platform. The officials would immediately give way and I would have the opportunity of addressing a well-prepared mass meeting. Before the police could have any inkling as to my whereabouts I would be finished and away; half an hour or an hour later the taxis would come rushing up, with the Inspector and his men eager, very eager, to serve their precious warrant.

I had a splendid campaign, which would not have been possible without the aid of those lodge officials. They thoroughly enjoyed the game of outwitting the police.

On leaving Durham I made for Fife. The boys there gave me a great reception at meeting after meeting. One of the best and most memorable was one in Buckhaven. My schedule had got knocked a bit groggy. I was three-quarters of an hour behind my time when I got into the meeting.

Jimmy Hope, one of my best friends in the East Fife area, and one of the most likeable and popular of our comrades, was holding the fort until I arrived. The hall was packed to suffocation. Every available inch of space was taken up. As I came on to the platform a roar of greeting rose from the hall to meet me.

When it died down Jimmy Hope said: " Well, auld Willie's here at last." He then went on: " The reformists say that we're just a lot of young irresponsibles. But, here's auld Willie, he's been in the fight as long as any o' them. The difference between him and them is, his brain has kept young and they've become fossilized."

This pawky reiteration of " auld Willie " had the audience rocking with laughter. I never rose to speak at any time or anywhere in a more cordial, happy and receptive atmosphere. And at this time, these men had been out on strike for over five months.

All over Fife it was the same. The spirit of the men, and of their womenfolk too, was undaunted—unconquerable. Everywhere the utmost activity around the food kitchens, the boot-repairing depots, etc. In Lochgelly, my shoes were soled and heeled but when the job was done, the Red Flag was worked on to each sole.

These days in the latter part of 1926 were great and inspiring ones to spend among the Fife miners. In the midst of it all, the question was continually being raised: " Why should there be two unions in Fife? Isn't it time we had unity? We're all fighting together, why shouldn't we be organized together?" When the strike ended, these questions remained to be answered. From all sides demands for unity came and so negotiations started for bringing about an amalgamation of the two unions, the County Union, of which Adamson was secretary, and the Reform Union of which Philip Hodge was secretary.

This unity was accomplished in 1927, Adamson remaining general secretary with Philip Hodge occupying a subsidiary position in the office. All went well for a month or two and then came the election for a new executive and for two organisers. Five Communists were nominated for the two organisers' positions. After some discussion three of them withdrew leaving two to contest against two of

Adamson's lieutenants. The Communists came out on top and Adamson contested the ballot.

A new ballot was taken and a still bigger majority was registered for the Communists, the same applied to the executive members. A majority of Communists and strong left wingers was elected to the executive. While this was going on a ballot was also being taken for the Scottish executive and officers.

Willie Allan, at that time secretary of the Lanarkshire Miners' Union, was nominated for Scottish secretary, while one of the Fife men who has since deserted the movement, was nominated for President. Both positions were won as well as a majority on the Scottish executive. But the new executive could not function until it was endorsed by a national conference which could only be called by the old executive.

This national conference was and is an annual affair, which the existing executive has the responsibility of calling. When the ballot went against them the old executive refused to convene the national conference—so the new executive officials could not take office. Month after month the fight went on, with more and more miners leaving the unions in disgust. Then the old officials of the Lanarkshire Miners' Union took the drastic step of expelling the very men who had been successful in the ballot for the Scottish executive.

Adamson, as representative of the Fife, Clackmannan and Kinross Miners' Union, had been given instructions by his executive to support the demand for the convening of the national conference. But, far from carrying out these instructions, he supported every decision of his colleagues on the old executive. The executive of the Fife Union had to take cognisance of this and was forced eventually to take action. Adamson was suspended from his office of secretary and the executive decided to take a ballot of the members on the question of his dismissal.

While the ballot was being taken, Adamson, seeing the result, gathered his lieutenants around him, and started a new union giving it the name of Fife, Kinross and Clackmannan Miners' Union. Just a simple transposition of the second and third names. The old Scottish executive accepted Adamson's union as the official body and disaffiliated the original one, thus cutting it off from association with the Miners' Federation of Great Britain. For it is only through the Scottish executive that the County unions in Scotland have their connections with the M.F.G.B. This, of course, was a great advantage to Adamson, as many miners who had no liking for him or for his methods, were nevertheless anxious to be in the official union and maintain contact with the English and Welsh miners.

These events continued throughout 1928 and in 1929 the United Mineworkers of Scotland was formed at a conference, representative of delegates from the Fife union, the expelled members and branches of the Lanarkshire Miners' Union, several branches from Ayrshire and several from the

Lothians. The aim of the U.M.S. was the unity
of all Scottish miners in one strong Scottish Miners'
Union, a demand that has been in the forefront of
all active rank-and-file movements for many years.
Six county unions in Scotland, each with its own
executive and officials had for long represented an
intolerable and costly anomaly, one that played
beautifully into the hands of the mineowners.

The U.M.S. started off with a fairly good membership in Lanarkshire as well as in Fife, although
the membership in other districts was merely
nominal. But through a series of unfortunate and
ill-conducted stoppages an impression was created
in Lanarkshire that the only concern of the organizers of the new union was to stop the pits regardless
of whether there was cause for it or not, and very
soon the membership fell away leaving the union for
all effective purposes with its only substantial base
in Fife.

During the 1926 strike and the events which
immediately followed a new and very active young
man had come to the fore. This was Alex Moffat,
of Lumphinnans, a small village lying between
Cowdenbeath and Lochgelly. Alex and his brother
Abe had both joined the Communist Party and
soon proved to be keen political thinkers. Abe for
a while played a subsidiary role in the movement,
but Alex soon became one of its most dominant
personalities.

Both brothers were appointed check-weighmen at
the Pee-Weep Pit but towards the end of 1929 they

were removed from their positions by sheriff's interdict at the instance of the Fife Coal Co. for having participated in, or having led, a strike of the miners at the pit.* A short time after Abe was appointed as an organizer of the U.M.S. and the sterling qualities that have since become so pronounced, commenced to evidence themselves.

Alex soon afterwards was elected to the Fife County Council where he has rendered distinguished service ever since. At the last two elections he has been returned unopposed. About the same time Jimmy Stewart, another U.M.S. stalwart, was elected to the Lochgelly Town Council and became one of the outstanding stalwarts in the area.

But the U.M.S., following the collapse of membership in Lanarkshire, was going through a very difficult period. Willie Allan, the general secretary, who had battled against heavy odds for a long time, resigned his post and took up other work in the movement. He is now check-weighman at the Cambois Colliery, Northumberland. He was followed as general secretary by Dave Proudfoot of Methil. Proudfoot was subject to periods of deep depression which had a very bad effect on both organizers and members.

During this period, the " paid " organisers got little more than the unemployed relief scale. Not

---

* Two years earlier, Andrew Jarvie, who by his energetic work had won the solid support of the Valleyfield miners, had been removed from his position of check-weighman at the Fife Coal Co.'s pit in Valleyfield, by the same process, a sheriff's interdict. The Fife Coal Co. doesn't like Communists.

only so, but often there was no money for them at the end of the week and they would have to wait for several days before anything at all was found for them. Added to this debts were accumulating on all sides. The outlook for the U.M.S. was black indeed.

In July 1931, the Seven-and-a-half-hour Act of the Labour Government came into operation. The Scottish mineowners threatened a heavy cut in wages to offset the proposed half-hour's reductions in working time.

We conducted a terrific campaign in Fife against any reduction in wages and for the seven-hour day as against the seven and a half. On the day before the seven and a half hours came legally into force, no decision had been arrived at on the question of wages. The mineowners were demanding a cut of 1s. 4d. per day.

On the Monday evening I had a mass meeting at Bowhill. We were making preparations for a strike the following day. The night-shift men who were at the meeting suggested remaining out that night. I advised them against this and persuaded them to go to work that night and to be ready for action the next day. I finished the meeting and returned to Lumphinnans where a real shock awaited me. The Scottish executive had sent out telegrams to all the County unions (official) branches advising them to continue working the eight-hour day, adding that negotiations on wages were still going on.

On receipt of this telegram the Cowdenbeath

branch of the County union decided unanimously against working an illegal 8-hour day and declared for an immediate strike, the night shift being instructed not to go down that night. From Kelty and Lochore came similar reports.

All were out and I had advised Bowhill to remain in. Accompanied by Alex Moffat I rushed off to the Bowhill pit. We got there just as the men were about to go down the pit. I explained the situation that had developed in the area and they immediately agreed to fall in line with the others, their only complaint being that I had made them go home and change into their pit clothes for nothing.

For four weeks almost ten thousand Fife miners carried on the fight, with the County officials doing everything possible to break the strike and to get the Fife Miners to work the illegal eight hours which they had succeeded in maintaining in the other parts of the Scottish coalfields.

At the end of that time the 7½ hours was operated with a wage-cut of 4½d. instead of the 1s. 4d. the companies had originally demanded. It was another great demonstration of the fighting qualities of the Fife miners, and it saved the situation for the whole of the Scottish coalfield.

In this strike Abe Moffatt demonstrated beyond any question his quality of leadership. He was a tower of strength, showing keen political insight on all problems that arose, and a well-balanced judgment that could be relied on at all times. When, therefore, a short time after, Proudfoot " packed in " as

General Secretary of the U.M.S. with the dismal prophecy that the union would be out of existence in three months the executive had no hesitation in selecting Abe for the job.

He took over the union when it was loaded with debt and when everything appeared to be at its worst. But he brought an entirely new spirit to the work. This had an especial effect on the very competent office manager who hitherto had had no opportunity to keep the books and finances in order. She seized the opportunity afforded her with both hands and made a complete change in the office routine. With Abe released from this side of the work he was able to get down to the job of reorganizing the whole apparatus of the union. Once more the organizers began to receive their wages, such as they were, with regularity. The heavy debt was tackled, until gradually, after a hard struggle, it was wiped out. Even while the debt was being cleared off it was occasionally possible to make a small addition to the wages of the organizers and then, as the debt was liquidated, this addition was made permanent.

Then came a time when the monthly balance sheet instead of showing a deficit showed a balance. Not a penny of debt and a balance being built up. All this was accomplished in a year, with the union stronger and more influential than it had ever been before. Thus was the dismal prophecy of Proudfoot confounded. In all the Fife pits the advice and leadership of the U.M.S. was sought on every question. When the County Union officials failed them—which happened frequently—they could always rely on the U.M.S. officials fighting for them and safeguarding their interests. The U.M.S. developed a fine team of leaders, the brothers Moffat with Jimmy Stewart, Alex Campbell and a number of other lads in West Fife. In East Fife were Jock McArthur, a brilliant and versatile comrade who, although comparatively young, had been long associated with the workers' movement, being one of those who helped to form the Scottish Labour College, under the leadership of John McLean, and Bob Eadie, who had been transferred from Lanark-shire.

I had the loyal support of all these comrades when I stood as parliamentary candidate for West Fife in 1929. In this election I polled some six thousand seven hundred odd votes, while Adamson, the sitting member retained the seat. In 1931 I stood again and despite the terrific landslide which washed Adamson and so many others out, I not only retained my 1929 vote but added a hundred or so to it.

Following this election, the influence of the U.M.S. continued to increase and its work to extend. Then came a new development that had far-reaching effects so far as the strengthening of Communist influence in the area was concerned. The campaign for workmen's inspectors was taken up by the U.M.S. The process to be carried out under the Act is as follows: a plebiscite is taken at the pit of the required number of names, ten per cent having to be obtained, a meeting of the men is then called and two inspectors are nominated. If more than two should be nominated a vote of the meeting is taken. The defeated nominees can then demand a ballot of the pit. When the campaign started the County union officials came out with every kind of unscrupulous attack upon the leaders of the U.M.S. and opposed tooth and nail the proposals for regular workmen's inspectors. When a plebiscite was being taken at the pit they tried to persuade the men not to participate. When they failed in this they endeavoured to get the Coal Companies to accept their nominees without a vote of the miners. This attempt was defeated by the U.M.S. who had the mass support of the miners and in consequence ballot votes were conducted at nearly all the pits in Fife for the election of workmen's inspectors. This was the course of events at all the principal pits in Fife with Adamson issuing leaflets and statements in the Press on his favourite topic, namely, " The Moscow agents who are out to disrupt the miners' organizations."

Anyone who challenged Adamson's " private ownership " of the miners' unions or of the West Fife constituency, both of which were his by "Divine Right", was immediately damned with bell, book and candle as Moscow agents. Moscow appeared to have no other reason for existence than to employ agents to disturb the peace of the Right Honorable Wm. Adamson.

But despite all his frenzied efforts to distract the attentions of the miners, his nominees were completely routed at all the leading pits in Fife. McArthur and Eadie became pit inspectors in East Fife, Alex Moffat, Jimmy Stewart and Alex Campbell in West Fife. Their inspections were and are carried out in the most thorough and painstaking fashion and have been the means not only of securing improvements in the pits and greater safety for the miners but also of stopping the working of overtime and other undesirable practices. But the fight around this issue of pit inspectors, apart from the invaluable work done by them, was an important factor in preparing the minds of the workers for the 1935 election.

Adamson, when he failed to stop the campaign, had made the issue quite clear—for his nominees or for the Communist nominees. Every kind of anti-Communist slander was circulated in the area in the desperate effort to defeat the U.M.S.

But there was such a contrast in service to the miners, between the U.M.S. nominees and his own, that all he succeeded in doing was to popularize Communism instead of discrediting it and thereby helping to prepare the way for his own final eclipse in the elections of 1935.

When the campaign for this election started all the boys were highly confident and ready to take on anything. Jock McArthur had been elected on to the Buckhaven Town Council and from that body was sent as representative to the Fife County

Council. Mrs. Stewart of Methilhill, an untiring vigorous fighter for the working class, had been elected to the District Council. Jimmy Stewart was standing for re-election for the Lochgelly Council in the November Municipal Elections, while Bob Selkirk and a young comrade named Fairlie were standing as Municipal candidates in Cowdenbeath.

Andrew Jarvie of Dunfermline, Jock Sutherland of Bowhill and Bob Eadie of Methilhill and Jimmy Hope of East Wemyss were all nominated for the County Council elections in December.

All this contributed to making the election campaign one of the most lively ever carried out in any constituency. Many comrades came in from outside to help and every one of them was an asset. Eight or nine cars were brought in by friends from outside, without which we would have been at a terrible disadvantage. Actually we could have utilized dozens more. There are about fifty villages in the constituency which is very scattered, and demands a most efficient transport service if it is to be covered as it should be on such occasions.

On November 5, the local elections took place. Jimmy Stewart came out on top in Lochgelly with a record vote of over 1,800. In Cowdenbeath where Selkirk and Fairlie were standing against two Labour men, two Moderates and two I.L.P.'ers (the latter refused to come to an understanding with us on the grounds that the ward was an I.L.P. ward) Selkirk and Fairlie came out on top, easy winners, with the two I.L.P.'ers at the bottom, the Moderates and Labour men in the middle.*

This was a good augury for my election and gave new encouragement and strength to the campaign. Wherever we went, even in what were considered the " backward " places, we found a hearty reception waiting for us and an eager desire to hear and understand our case. So by the time the campaign ended, everyone was confident of the result. In the sheriff's office in Dunfermline where the votes were being counted, there was consternation when it became obvious that I was in. Adamson's agent went out to the corridor to break the news to the old man.

" It's not possible," Adamson exclaimed. " Demand a recount." The agent tried to persuade him against this course, but he would not be persuaded. It wasn't possible that he could be defeated. When he at last realized the truth, that the constituency didn't belong to him any longer, he disappeared from the scene.

But he wasn't the only one to be displeased at my victory. When the sheriff's clerk had the final figures, the sheriff was brought in and the figures

* In the County Council elections which took place in December we had two further victories. Andrew Jarvie won the Culross division, which embraces his own stronghold, Valleyfield, and Blairhill.

In Bowhill young John Sutherland, who stood for the first time, thoroughly defeated a renegade Communist. Although youthful, he had deservedly won the confidence of the Bowhill miners, and has done a great service in putting a finish to the career of his opponent.

were handed over to him. In the two previous elections with Adamson the victor in one case and Mr. Chas. Milne (Conservative) in the other, the sheriff on receipt of the figures had shaken hands with the victor and congratulated him on his election. He then invited the victor to accompany him whilst he read out the figures and whilst votes of thanks were given and short speeches made.

But on this occasion the sheriff looked at the figures, but he didn't look at me. No.

Without a word or a glance, he walked out to make the public declaration of the poll. I followed. He got on the platform, read out the figures, turned, and walked off, leaving me standing there alone. Alone on the platform, but not alone otherwise. There in front of me was a dense mass of workers, in the forefront of which was Peter Kerrigan and Aitken Ferguson, cheering again and again in the wild enthusiasm of victory.

One of the most important factors in the election campaign had been the strike of the Valleyfield miners and the feeling that was aroused around this strike.* In the middle of October the Valleyfield

---

* The strike lasted for thirteen weeks, and was one of the most solid and longest pit strikes in the history of Fife. The men were fighting to return on the basis of the status quo. The Fife Coal Co. declared that there would be no negotiations till the men returned to work and that they must return on the basis of a Dirt Scale. After the election I wrote to the Scottish Executive of the Miners and the M.F.G.B. Executive. They were prepared to intervene but they could only do so if they were invited to participate by the County Union. This invitation was not forthcoming. Adamson blocked the road to any reinforcements for the strikers. I then

miners had struck against an attempt of the Fife Coal Co. to introduce a " Dirt Scale " of 44 lbs. per hutch. This affected about 90 strippers and meant an actual reduction in their wages; when they stopped work it meant that the whole pit, about 600 men and boys, were out. Practically all of these men were in Adamson's union, but instead of getting support from him they found that he was for acceptance of the Dirt Scale. The men at once angrily repudiated this.

Then the union law agent paid a visit to Valleyfield for the purpose of informing the strikers that the company were legally entitled to enforce a Dirt Scale. This only increased the anger of the men. Later on the County Union executive met and decided not to support the strike. By this time the strikers had invited Abe Moffat and the other leaders of the U.M.S. to assist them with the strike.

went to the Ministry of Mines and got the officials there interested. I followed this up by putting down a question on the matter. When this question appeared I had a further meeting with the officials of the Mines Department and agreed to withdraw my question pending further negotiations of which they would take charge.

Early in January an official of the Department went to Fife to meet the representative of the Fife Coal Co., and the County Union. As a result of this meeting a formula was submitted and agreed to which provided for a return to work on the basis of the status quo, with the understanding that the negotiations would immediately start on the question at issue. The men being prepared to put forward proposals to eliminate the need for Dirt Scale. Having accepted the proposals the men returned to work on 13th January. They returned to work as solid as they were when they first came out on strike, and more than ever determined to fight against any attempt to impose a Dirt Scale on the pit.

Abe and the others made a campaign around the company's other pits, and week by week groups of strikers were allocated for collections at these pits. A ready response was given to the collections and soon a communal feeding centre was in full swing in Valleyfield.

During the election campaign, Valleyfield became one of the outstanding issues at all our meetings. The Labour Party policy in International affairs had declared for sanctions against the aggressor. The reactionary forces were for a free hand for the aggressor. Yet here in Fife the Labour candidate instead of fighting to defend the unions against the glaring aggression of the Fife Coal Co., was actually pursuing the line of open reaction, a free hand for the aggressor against his own union members.

Adamson's conduct in connection with the Valleyfield dispute was the decisive factor in the West Fife electoral contest.

The election resulted in a great victory for the Communist Party, a victory that had only been rendered possible by years of hard work on the part of a devoted band of comrades, sparing neither time nor energy in the fight to advance the cause of the working class. It was an expression of confidence in the Communist Party and in myself as its representative, confidence that we will at all times put the interests of the workers before all else.

APPENDIX A.

AS a new Member, I have been given advice by many older Members of the House, and I will endeavour to avail myself of it in so far as it is consistent with what I am supposed to do as the representative of a great working-class constituency. I have been advised that, on rising to address the House, one should make at least a reference to the preceding speech. I am sorry that in this case I cannot accept that advice. I cannot tolerate such flippancy, coming from a constituency where the medical officer last year could issue a report that 50 per cent of the children attending the schools were suffering from disease or defects. I have seen the harrowing effects of the most terrible poverty and suffering in the homes of the people, and I am not of the temper that takes these things lightly.

In the King's Speech are many questions that must be dealt with frankly. There is the conflict in Abyssinia. I want to bring out clearly the issue that is involved, for some of my hon. Friends for whom I have great regard have won applause from the other side of the House on this question. I hope I may never see the day when I win applause from the opposite side of the House. I am concerned with the fact that confusion is being created on this vital question, and is being used by supporters of the Government. The great Labour movement in this country stands for rigid opposition to robber aggression on principle. These benches represent support for the Abyssinians, a colonial people, in the fight they are making to maintain their independence. That is the vital difference between this side of the House and the other. Questions of sanctions and the application of sanctions cannot be allowed to confuse this difference.

The leader of the Liberal party yesterday gave an exhibition of the most deliberate self-deception on this point. I do not mind his deceiving himself, but I object to his trying to deceive others. He said that the Foreign Secretary's speech at Geneva represented a change of policy. It represented nothing of the sort, but only a continuation of a policy that has been pursued by the National Government, adapted to a new situation. It represented the brazen hypocrisy that has appeared time and time again in the utterances of representatives of the National Government. How any man could make such a speech, I do not know, with a National Government imposing its military control over Egypt, with the iron heel of British Imperialism crushing down the Indians. If there is to be independence for Abyssinia, for which we stand, then there must be independence for Egypt, for India, for all colonial peoples, and the right of the colonial peoples to work out their own destiny associated with and assisted by the more advanced Western peoples.

Is the National Government co-operating with the League of Nations? Reference was made by the Leader of the Opposition to dualism, but that word is being used now to create an entirely wrong impression. You can easily have an immediate programme and an ultimate aim. The National Government are pursuing not a dual policy but are playing a double game, and are preparing, if the opportunity presents itself, for what the Americans call a " double cross." The National Government are ready at any moment to double cross the League of Nations and to double cross Abyssinia if it can make a deal with Italy. The Foreign Secretary when he made his speech was pursuing exactly the same policy as the previous Foreign Secretary when he was handling the Japanese affair.

Never until this situation arose did we see in the National Government any passionate desire for the League of Nations. When Japan invaded Manchuria, the then Foreign Secretary did not support the League of Nations against Japan; he became the spokesman for Japan against the League of Nations. Why? Because he told you that he was trying to get a deal with Japan that would guarantee British railway interests in Manchuria and China. The passion for the League of Nations only arose when British Imperial and financial interests were threatened in the North of Africa. The attitude of the National Government towards the League of Nations is to utilize it as far as it can in order to force Italy to make a deal for the safeguarding of British interests in the Sudan and Egypt.

When the right hon. Gentleman the Member for Warwick and Leamington (Mr. Eden) was in Moscow last year, he was in a real atmosphere of peace. [*Interruption.*] Yes, war does not come from the heart of human beings; it comes as a consequence of the greed for territory and trading profits. Take away the incentive of the element of profit and you take away the incentive for war. In Soviet Russia there is no desire for any territory outside their own. Stalin has said that they do not covet an inch of anybody else's territory, but will not give up an inch of their own. For the building of Socialism they must have peace, and so a peace policy is being pursued. While the right hon. Member for Warwick and Leamington was there in what he himself declared to be a real peace atmosphere, the Foreign Secretary was grovelling before the butcher of Berlin. The door was slammed shut and you had the spectacle of the British Foreign Secretary waiting until he was given permission to enter. Did that produce peace or peace discussions? It produced the German Naval Pact, drove France away from Britain into the arms of Italy, and gave Italy the opportunity, as a result of the unsettling of the whole European situation, to make an attack upon Abyssinia.

I challenge anyone to deny that had there been no pro-German policy there would have been no war against Abyssinia. The German Naval Pact was the coping stone on the remilitarization of Germany. There is a Cenotaph in Whitehall, erected to a million young Britishers done to death in Flanders and on other fronts. There are a million more broken men. I will take you round some of the asylums, I will take you to the hospitals. They were sent to die to destroy German militarism, which was menacing civilization. But now German militarism is erected stronger than ever before. Will hon. Gentlemen take down the Cenotaph? The rearming of Germany is a serious question, and has brought a menace to the whole of civilization.

Now the scene has changed. The one-time Foreign Secretary, Hitler's Man Friday, is now at the Home Office. We are getting a German invasion of London. Is any hon. Member prepared to say that this has nothing to do with *bona fide* football and sport? [*Interruption.*] Hon. Gentlemen may laugh, but do not let them forget that this invasion may be the forerunner of a different invasion. Whatever animates the German militarist, whoever they would desire to crush at the moment, there is one thing will always stand before them, and that is the hope that the day may come when they may crush the Imperialists of Britain and invade London. An hon. Member with a touch of humour said that if you put men on to making armaments, 16s. in the £ will go in wages. If you put men to dig holes in the sand, 20s. in the £ will go in wages. If hon. Members are so engaged about armaments, why not get men and boys piling up metal on each side of the House and we can settle our quarrels by throwing scrap-iron at each other.

You cannot ever hope to combat the war spirit that has remained in Germany by building up armaments. That can only be done by denouncing the German Naval Treaty, and then, associated with that greatest peace power in the world, the Soviet Union, associated with and supporting the Franco-Soviet peace pact, and around this building all the peace nations of Europe. If you have fifty nations co-operating for peace and carrying forward a steady policy of peace and disarmament, through their economic and financial power you can force the other nations to disarm also. If you use your economic and financial power Germany and Japan will be forced to disarm. The National Government, composed of Tory die-hards with the discredited remnants of other parties thrown in, will never lead the fight for peace.

What of defence? Have you defended the miners' families in Wales, Lancashire, on the North-East Coast and in Scotland? Have you defended these places—go and look at them—which give the appearance of a country that has been devastated by the enemy? Have you defended the miners? There were over 1,000 men killed in the pits last year and nearly 200,000 injured. Have you defended them? Come with me to the mining villages, and, day after day, you can see the terrible tragedy of the pit, and the tragedy of the miners' homes. Have you defended the unemployed? We have heard about the means test. Yesterday the hon. Member for Bridgeton (Mr. Maxton) drew attention to the gyrations of hon. Gentlemen opposite in connection with the means test during the Election. There was not one Member on the other side prepared to stand up for the means test as it was being operated in any industrial constituency in the country. Why? Because of the terrible effects the means test was having upon men, women and children in the country. Not one of them would defend it or stand for it. When pressure is brought to bear upon the matter, we hear some flippant talk about going to change it. You are going to change it, but are you going to compensate in any way for the evil you have done during the past four years?

I have heard of hundreds of cases, but one of the most outstanding in my mind at the moment is that of one of the heroes who came back from the war paralysed. He has lain in bed since the end of the war and has never moved. Do you remember the promise we made as to the treatment that these heroes were to receive? Do you remember how the duke and the worker were to walk along the road hand-in-hand, with roses on every side and happiness lying close at hand? Here is a paralysed man lying in bed. His boy grows to manhood—he is twenty-one years of age—and gets a job. The means test is operated in that home. He is persuaded to leave home and live with relatives so that the family income shall not be interfered with. He leaves his bed-ridden father and weeping mother and goes to his new home. He cannot eat; he cannot sleep. Despair settles upon him, and in a week comes the end—suicide. He is driven to death by the means test, as thousands of others have been done to death. Were you anxious for them? Are you going to change it because you have seen the ghastly work which you have done? I have seen it, and I cannot forget it. You have not defended the unemployed and the mothers and the children. It is all very well for the Prime Minister, in his introductory speech, to say that on the question of maternity and midwifery there will not be any need for political opposition. It is a very serious problem and one which is dear to his heart. The Chief Medical Officer in his report last year drew attention to the fact that we were making no headway against maternal mortality. Where does the trouble come from? It comes from low wages and low unemployment relief. The mothers and children have to suffer. You may pay tribute to, or worship, the Madonna and Child, but day after day you are doing the Madonna and Child to death.

On this side of the House we represent and speak for the workers of this country, the men who toil and sweat. [Hon. Members: " So do we."] Oh, you do speak for the workers, do you? [Hon. Members: " Yes."] All right. We shall see. The leader of the miners says that theirs is the hardest, most dangerous and poorest paid job in the country. Is there anybody who will deny it? The miners make a demand. They ballot for it, and the ballot is a record, and we who speak for and on behalf of the miners demand an increase of 2s. a day for the miners. That is how we speak for the miners. Now it is your turn. Speak now. Two shillings a day for the miners. Speak, you who claim to represent the miners. We say not a penny for armaments. It is a crime against the people of this country to spend another penny on armaments. Every penny we can get should be on wages for the miners, towards the health and well-being of the mothers and the children and adequate pensions for the aged and infirm. Ten shillings a week. I would like the Noble Lady to receive only 10s. and then she would change her tune. Last night the Chancellor of the Exchequer was meeting some friends, and they were having a dinner, the cost of which was 35s. per head. Thirty-five shillings per head for a dinner, and 10s. a week for an aged man or woman who has given real service to this country and has worked in factory or mine. We require every penny we can get in order to make life better for the working class. If the £7,000,000,000 which we spent during the war in ruin and destruction had been spent in making life brighter and better for the people of this country what a difference it would have made.

I would make an earnest appeal to hon. Members of the House who have not yet become case-hardened in iniquity. The National Government are travelling the road of 1914, which will surely lead to another and more terrible war, and to the destruction of civilization. Are hon. Members going to follow them down that road? The party which is represented on these benches, from which, at the present moment, I am an outcast, has set itself a task of an entirely different character, that of travelling along the road of peace and progress and of spending all that can be spent in making life higher and better for all. We invite those of you who are prepared to put service to a great cause before blind leadership of miserable pygmies who are giving a pitiful exhibition by masquerading as giants, to put first service not to a National Government such as is presented before us, but to a Labour Government drawing towards itself all the very best and most active and progressive elements from all parties and constituting itself, as a consequence, a real people's Government concerned with the complete reconstruction of this country, with genuine co-operation with the other peace nations for preserving world peace, a Government that follows the road of peace and progress. I make an appeal even while I give a warning. Do not try to stop us on the road along which we are travelling. Do not try to block the road by the meshes of legal entanglements or by Fascist gangs. Do not try it, lest an evil day come upon you and you have to pay a price far beyond any present reckoning.

APPENDIX B.

ON December 29, 1935, the United Mineworkers of Scotland held a conference in Dunfermline where a decision was taken to disband the Union and advise all members to join up immediately in the county unions associated with the Mineworkers' Federation of Great Britain. The resolution embodying this decision was as follows:—

" In accordance with the overwhelming majority ballot vote decision of the members of the U.M.S. and in light of the very important fight conducted by the Mineworkers' Federation of Great Britain around the fight for a 2s. wage increase for all miners, along with the important decision of the Executive Committee of the National Union of Scottish Mine-workers in turning down the Scottish mineowners' proposals to discuss district agreements in place of a national agreement, the Executive Committee of the U.M.S. has decided that the time has come when it is necessary to take the most decisive step for achieving unity by advising all members to immediately join up in the county unions.

" We believe that this decision will be greeted by thousands of miners all over the coalfield as an important step forward in building complete unity of the miners, and a further demonstration to the Government and the coalowners that the miners are rallying behind the M.F.G.B. and are determined to obtain wage increases on a national basis."

INDEX

Lightning Source UK Ltd.
Milton Keynes UK
UKOW05f0604050717
304716UK00001B/80/P